Change from Within

A Journal of Exercises and Meditations to Transform, Empower, and Reconnect

Elke Elouise Taylor

Skyhorse Publishing

Skyhorse Publishing books may be purchased in bulk at special discounts for sales promotion, corporate gifts, fund-raising, or educational purposes. Special editions can also be created to specifications. For details, contact the Special Sales Department, Skyhorse Publishing, 307 West 36th Street, 11th Floor, New York, NY 10018 or info@ skyhorsepublishing.com.

Skyhorse® and Skyhorse Publishing® are registered trademarks of Skyhorse Publishing, Inc.®, a Delaware corporation.

Visit our website at www.skyhorsepublishing.com.

10 9 8 7 6 5 4 3 2 1

Library of Congress Cataloging-in-Publication Data is available on file.

Cover design by Jane Sheppard

Print ISBN: 978-1-5107-2908-7

Printed in China

You are your own soul mate

ENLOVENMENT

There's a big, beautiful shift in global consciousness going on. If you've felt that inner niggle of dissatisfaction, a suspicion that you're just skimming the surface of life, or a yearning for a deeper connection with who you really are and all you can be, then you are being called.

A powerful life force energy flows through all of us, connecting and uniting everything. In this "age of mind" we live in, we've lost sight of this vital connection. We've forgotten that we are life force energy in physical form. Another name for this life force energy is love—authentic love in its myriad of forms. Enlightenment means to be full of light, but a better word for this self-actualization would be en-love-nment. Want to know who you really are and what you came here to do? Start by becoming the lover you were meant to be.

Embracing all of who you are isn't just some esoteric spiritual practice with no real-world use (what would be the point?). All of our fears and doubts take hold because we don't trust ourselves. And you cannot trust yourself if you are not wholly connected to yourself. On top of that, all creation begins on the inside. When our thoughts, feelings, and beliefs align with this life force energy, we quickly and easily manifest the things we desire. When you stand present and own all of who you are, not only do stress and anxiety become a thing of the past, you'll also start living to your full potential. What's not to love?

MASTERY

Unfortunately, it doesn't matter how smart you are or how hard you try—unhealed emotional wounds distort the connection with life force energy. If you're feeling like there's something wrong with you, suffering a lack of motivation, or stuck in sabotaging patterns, then old wounds are already affecting your life. The first step towards embracing who we really are is healing and transforming our wounds and insecurities. The good news is that healing the emotional body isn't rocket science. The not-so-good news is that the road to emotional mastery can only be walked by going deeply within, and this won't always feel good.

Based on an Intuitive Healing practice I developed from ten years of research, *Change from Within* is full of practical, easy-to-follow tools and processes that peel away the layers blocking you from fully connecting with your authentic self. The exercises in the first half of the journal focus on healing wounds, insecurities, and beliefs, showing you how to transform them into clarity and wisdom. Only after doing this necessary internal "cleaning house" do we shift focus to strengthening your connection to the greater part of you that is life force energy, laying the foundations of healthy self-esteem, self-worth, and self-empowerment.

Following the body's natural biorhythms, the journal is divided into twelve weeks of short daily meditations and longer weekend homework. To get the most out of this, do the entire process once, followed by a six-week "self-help break," bringing what you learned into your day-to-day life. Then redo the journal a second time, working the process on a deeper level. I'd also suggest completing *Change from Within* with your partner or friends. You don't want to read each other's notes, but support one another and share insights as you go. Because, whether you know it or not, we are *all* in this together.

Now hold onto your hats beautiful people because we're about to go on an adventure, an adventure into the unique being that is you!

I can't promise smooth sailing,
but I can make you a better sailor.

Week 1 (Monday)

Time required: 5–10 minutes

In order to make any changes in your life, we first have to look at where you are now. On a scale of 1–10 (1 being "I seriously hate my life" and 10 being "I'm-so-happy-why-did-I-buy-this-book?") how would you rate your life today?

_____

Every Monday you're going to give yourself this simple life evaluation. Be honest but don't be disheartened. A realistic starting point is essential for clearing the path to where we wish to be.

Every weekday, find a few minutes where you won't be interrupted. You could be in bed or on the bus; it doesn't matter, so long as you won't be distracted. Place one hand over your diaphragm, the space between the belly button and the sternum, and close your eyes. Take three deep breaths, bringing your awareness down into your body to the space behind your hand. Then say out loud, "I feel . . . "

You can use a metaphor or nonemotional word—the most important thing is becoming conscious of how you feel. Once you've named everything, write down the unpleasant emotions. Don't judge or analyze, just write it down.

_____

_____

_____

_____

Week 1 affirmation: "I make a promise to myself to find a few minutes every day to do my inner work, because I am worth it!" When I say this out loud three times, I feel . . . (write down the positive and not-so-positive emotions)

_____

_____

_____

_____

Week 1 (Tuesday)

Time required: 5 minutes

Place a hand over your diaphragm and close your eyes. Take three deep breaths, bringing your awareness down into your body to the space behind where your hand is. Then say out loud, "I feel . . . " (Name everything you feel but only write down the uncomfortable emotions.)

_____

_____

_____

_____

We're capable of feeling many things at once; however, you might struggle to name more than a few feelings when you first begin so I've put an emotional cheat sheet at the end of the journal to help you out.

Week 1 affirmation: "I make a promise to myself to find a few minutes every day to do my inner work, because I am worth it!" When I say this out loud three times, I feel . . . (write down the positive and not-so-positive emotions)

_____

_____

_____

_____

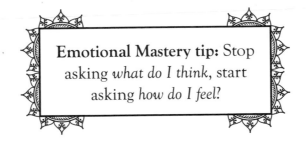

Emotional Mastery tip: Stop asking *what do I think*, start asking *how do I feel?*

Week 1 (Wednesday)

Time required: 5 minutes

Place a hand over your diaphragm and close your eyes. Take three deep breaths, bringing your awareness down to the space behind your hand. Then say out loud, "I feel . . . " (Name everything you feel but only write down the uncomfortable emotions.)

_____

_____

_____

_____

For this exercise, we only write down the uncomfortable emotions because these are the ones that need to be healed and transformed.

Week 1 affirmation: "I make a promise to myself to find a few minutes every day to do my inner work, because I am worth it!" When I say this out loud three times, I feel . . . (write down the positive and not-so-positive emotions)

_____

_____

_____

_____

Notes & Ideas:

_____

_____

_____

_____

_____

_____

_____

_____

_____

Week 1 (Thursday)

Time required: 5 minutes

Place a hand over your diaphragm, close your eyes. Take three deep breaths, breathing down into your diaphragm. Then say out loud, "I feel . . . " (Name everything you feel but only write down the uncomfortable emotions.)

_____

_____

_____

_____

Say the following out loud for each uncomfortable emotion you've written down above:

I feel . . . (uncomfortable emotion).
I allow myself to feel . . . (same emotion).

Naming "negative" emotions out loud brings them to the light of consciousness. Try not to just say the word robotically, but really own how you feel.

Week 1 affirmation: "I make a promise to myself to find a few minutes every day to do my inner work, because I am worth it!" When I say this out loud three times, I feel . . . (write down the positive and not-so-positive emotions this brings up)

_____

_____

_____

_____

Notes & Ideas:

_____

_____

_____

_____

_____

Week 1 (Friday)

Time required: 5 minutes

Place a hand over your diaphragm, close your eyes. Take three deep breaths, breathing deeply into your diaphragm. Then say out loud, "I feel . . . " (Name everything you feel but only write down the uncomfortable emotions.)

_____

_____

_____

_____

Then say out loud:

I allow myself to feel (name the uncomfortable emotions) . . .

You might think allowing something will only make it worse, when the opposite is actually true. This process is opening a connection with unhealed wounds so they can be transformed. If you feel resistance to allowing how you feel, add resistance to the list of emotions to process . . . because we're clever like that.

Week 1 affirmation: "I make a promise to myself to find a few minutes every day to do my inner work, because I am worth it!" When I say this out loud three times, I feel . . .

_____

_____

_____

_____

Notes & Ideas:

_____

_____

_____

_____

_____

You master your emotions, not control them. Trying to control your emotions would be like trying to control the ocean.

WEEKEND WORDS OF WISDOM

The first weekend's homework is like a full medical exam for the emotional body. Everyone has an aspect of their life they struggle with more than others—for some it's a fulfilling job, others a loving relationship. Whatever part of your life you wish to see the biggest change in, give it extra attention as you work through the exercises. You will come to see this "Achilles' heel" as your greatest teacher, teaching you authentic love.

Heads up: When you first begin to pay attention to how you feel, it may seem like things get worse before they get better. This process isn't making things worse; it's just making you aware of how much emotional baggage you've been carrying around.

YOUR MOST IMPORTANT RELATIONSHIP

Your relationship with yourself is the single most important relationship you have; yet sadly, it's the one most of us neglect. Taking time to understand who you are and what makes you tick isn't selfish, it's self-respect. This part of your inner transformation focuses on how you feel about yourself—not your physical body, even though it's connected—who you are as a person. When you have quiet moments alone or wake up in the middle of the night, how do you feel? If you can only name a few feelings, pay attention during these moments and add them to this list.

Heads up: In order to feel whole, we have to embrace all aspects of ourselves: both the light and the dark. Have the courage to name those traits or parts of yourself that, up until now, you may have been hiding or ashamed of.

_____

_____

_____

_____

When you think about where you are in your life right now, how does this feel? Be honest!

_____

_____

_____

_____

If where you are right now is exactly where you will be in five years' time, how does this make you feel? (If you had a slight panic attack reading that sentence, you're not alone.)

_____

_____

_____

_____

_____

Do you understand that, if you don't start making changes now, your life will look exactly the same in five years? I'm not trying to upset you, we're going to use these unpleasant emotions as motivation to start making some changes.

YOUR DIVINE PHYSICAL SELF

Strip down and stand in front of a mirror naked. What? I said it wasn't rocket science, I didn't say changing from within would be easy! Time to step up and get your naked-assed self in front of a mirror (you can ease the nightmare with some low light or candles, if that helps). Take some calming breaths and then look at yourself. Really look at yourself. You know the adage, "you've got to love yourself before you can love another," well, self-love begins right here. This exercise may be confronting, but it's also powerfully healing. The bigger the resistance, the greater the opportunity for transformation and growth, so be brave!

When I look at my body in the mirror, I feel . . . (write down the positive and not-so-positive emotions)

_____

_____

_____

_____

_____

Put your clothes back on and take a look at the list above. How critical or rejecting are you being of this manifestation of life force energy in physical form? Do you understand what an amazing feat of engineering your body is? We inhabit one of the most incredible and complex forms of life, and it's time to start appreciating it for the gift that it really is. Looking back in the mirror (you can keep your clothes on) start naming, then write down, all of the things your body does perfectly well that you don't really think about: the miles your feet walk, the blood your heart pumps, the food your stomach turns into energy. (Use Notes & Ideas space if you need more lines.)

_____

_____

_____

_____

Think of a child learning a new sport—there's the coach who berates, and the coach who encourages. Which one do you think gets the best long-term results? If you want to make any changes to what you see in the mirror, you're not going to be able to attain and maintain the body you desire unless you're coming from a place of love.

CONSCIOUS RELATIONSHIPS

Did you know how we connect with others is a mirror to how well we connect with ourselves? If you feel unheard or misunderstood by friends or family, then you're not listening to or understanding yourself. If you feel invisible or disrespected, then you're not seeing or respecting yourself. See your relationship with other people as perfectly reflecting where you need to do some work on your relationship with yourself. The more challenging the external relationship, the more inner work you need to do.

We start with your primary intimate relationship. How does your partner make you feel? If you're single or a loved one has passed, how does that make you feel?*

_____

_____

_____

_____

Then look at your closest family. How do you feel about these relationships?

_____

_____

_____

_____

Now look at friendships. How do you feel about the friendships you have in your life?

_____

_____

_____

_____

_____

In the week ahead as you spend time with or think about these people, pay attention to how you feel, adding any "negative" emotions to your list.

*Grief or a broken heart is what happens when love turns into resistance. If you are grieving, go below the pain into the resistance and process this in the weeks ahead. Once you drop the resistance, the love that was there will reemerge, transformed. Grief is a tricky beast, so be gentle on yourself.

CONSCIOUS CREATION

Contrary to what you might think, our career and finances aren't about the bling and the buck$. It's a good indicator of internal beliefs, often subconscious, around prosperity and abundance. Life force energy, the same energy that created universes, flows through every cell in our bodies. This energy is pure abundance consciousness and it is our natural state. If you are not doing fulfilling and enriching work, then you are not living the authentic expression of who you really are.

You've no doubt heard of the Law of Attraction. Scientists agree that at the most basic level, everything is made up of vibrating energy. What they're yet to cotton on to (give them time) is that what we are vibrating internally through our thoughts, feelings, and beliefs creates through attraction our external physical world. Most people are unconsciously creating their external reality because they've not taken care of their inner world, and wonder why they're unhappy?! The exercises around this aspect of your transformation are designed to clean up your internal vibration, helping you become a conscious creator.

If you're not passionate about how you support yourself, how do you feel when you're at work? If you're unemployed, how does this make you feel? If you work part-time as, say, a working mother, how does this feel?

_____

_____

_____

_____

_____

If you're not sure how you feel, start to pay attention during your workday, then write it down.

If your finances aren't in the place you'd like them to be, check your bank balance right now. Looking at this number, how do you feel? (I get this is asking the friggin' obvious, but it's important to name everything.)

_____

_____

_____

_____

_____

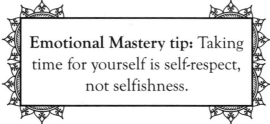

Emotional Mastery tip: Taking time for yourself is self-respect, not selfishness.

Notes & Ideas:

_____

_____

_____

_____

_____

_____

_____

We are emotional beings, yet we spend ten-plus years in school being taught how to think and never one lesson in how to feel. It's time to change this!

Week 2 (Monday)

On a scale of 1–10 (1 being "my life is crap" and 10 "life is fabulous, dahling"), where do you feel your life is at right now?

_____

Find a few minutes where you won't be interrupted. Place a hand over your diaphragm and close your eyes. Take three deep breaths, bringing your focus into the space behind your hand. Say out loud, "I feel . . ." (Name everything but only write down the uncomfortable emotions.)

_____
_____
_____
_____

Say out loud:

> I allow myself to feel (name the uncomfortable emotions above) . . .
> I give myself permission to feel (name the uncomfortable emotions from above) . . .

"Permit" and "allow" have slightly different energies and therefore emotional hooks. "Allow" is to yield or flow along with things. By "permitting," your mind (hopefully) knows you're in charge and that you give consent to feel uncomfortable.

Week 2 affirmation: "It is my intention to know who I really am and all I can be." When I say this out loud three times, I feel . . .

_____
_____
_____
_____

On your first go-through of this journal you may not vibe with all the affirmations—just be honest and write down how you feel. As you work through the process in the weeks and months ahead, you will become more aligned with the words.

Week 2 (Tuesday)

Time required: about 5 minutes

Place a hand over your diaphragm and close your eyes. Take three deep breaths, bringing your focus into the space behind your hand. Say out loud, "I feel . . . " (Name everything but only write down the uncomfortable emotions.)

_____

_____

_____

_____

Then say out loud:

> I allow myself to feel (repeat the phrase as you name each uncomfortable emotion from above) . . .
> I give myself permission to feel (repeat the phrase as you name each uncomfortable emotion from above)

Week 2 affirmation: "It is my intention to know who I really am and all I can be." When I say this out loud three times, I feel . . .

_____

_____

_____

_____

Notes & Ideas:

_____

_____

_____

_____

_____

_____

_____

Week 2 (Wednesday)

Time required: about 5 minutes

Place a hand over your diaphragm and close your eyes. Take three deep breaths, bringing your focus to the space behind your hand. Say out loud, "I feel . . . " (Name everything but only write down the uncomfortable emotions.)

_____

_____

_____

_____

Speak the Intuitive Healing process out loud:

I allow myself to feel (repeat the phrase as you name each uncomfortable emotion from above) . . .

I give myself permission to feel (repeat this phrase as you name each uncomfortable emotion from above) . . .

I accept that I feel (repeat as you name each uncomfortable emotion from above) . . .

Contrary to what the sabotaging mind may tell you, acceptance won't make things worse. Acceptance is simply an acknowledgment of where you are at.

Week 2 affirmation: "It is my intention to know who I really am and all I can be." When I say this out loud three times, I feel . . .

_____

_____

_____

_____

Notes & Ideas:

_____

_____

_____

Week 2 (Thursday)

Time required: about 5 minutes

Place a hand over your diaphragm and close your eyes. Take three deep breaths, bringing your focus to the space behind your hand. Say out loud, "I feel . . . " (Name everything but only write down the uncomfortable emotions.)

_____

_____

_____

_____

I allow myself to feel (speak this phrase out loud, naming each uncomfortable emotion) . . .

I give myself permission to feel (speak this phrase out loud, naming each uncomfortable emotion). . .

I accept that I feel (speak this phrase out loud, naming each uncomfortable emotion) . . .

Many people struggle to accept unpleasant emotions. This honest acknowledgment of how you feel is necessary to heal and transform our more challenging emotions.

Week 2 affirmation: "It is my intention to know who I really am and all I can be." When I say this out loud three times, I feel . . .

_____

_____

_____

_____

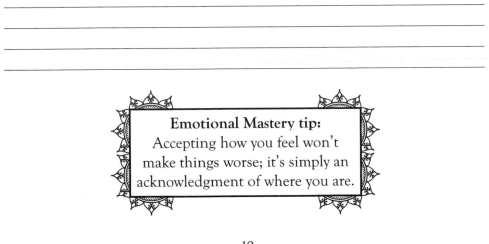

Emotional Mastery tip:
Accepting how you feel won't make things worse; it's simply an acknowledgment of where you are.

Week 2 (Friday)

Time required: about 5 minutes

Place a hand over your diaphragm and close your eyes. Take three deep breaths, bringing your focus to the space behind your hand. Say out loud, "I feel . . . " (Name everything but only write down the uncomfortable emotions.)

_____

_____

_____

_____

To be clear: in the very first step of this process, "I feel . . . " say out loud EVERYTHING, pleasant and unpleasant, but only write down the unpleasant. In the next steps only speak (and process) the unpleasant emotions, because these are what need to be healed and transformed. Unless I say otherwise, work this way in the days and weeks ahead.

I allow myself to feel . . .
I give myself permission to feel . . .
I accept that I feel . . .

It will feel like a weight lifts off your shoulders when you truly accept just where you are.

Week 2 affirmation: "It is my intention to know who I really am and all I can be." When I say this out loud three times, I feel . . .

_____

_____

_____

_____

It's _really_ important to pay attention to how you feel as you say the affirmation. You can think and say all the positive things you like, but if your feelings aren't also in alignment, you'll never create it.

WEEKEND WORDS OF WISDOM

Not accepting how we feel is like walking into the emergency room and refusing to tell the doctors where it hurts, but still expecting them to make you better. Acceptance doesn't mean putting up with something (which only leads to resentment); it is the honest acknowledgment of "this is where I'm at right now." Just like a GPS can't give directions if it doesn't know the starting point, only from the place of accepting how we feel, can we begin to map a path to how we wish to feel.

YOUR MOST IMPORTANT RELATIONSHIP

Well done on getting through the first two weeks of your transformation! Out loud, say, "Well done, me!" How does that feel?

_____

_____

Do you realize it's no one else's job to make sure you're happy and fulfilled? It's your job! As a matter of fact, it's your most important job. So far in life, how well have you been doing this job?

_____

_____

The most powerful way to strengthen our relationship with ourselves is to start taking time for ourselves. The good news is you are already doing this with the weekday 5–10 minute Intuitive Healing process. In the week ahead you're going to take this even further by scheduling "self-time." At the moment, how much time do you have for art and creativity, play and adventure, or whatever it is that makes your heart sing? My guess is not very much.

_____

_____

Get out your planner and look at your week ahead. Where can you find two "self" hours? Just after you drop the kids off at school? When you first leave work? If this area is your Achilles' heel (I'm looking at you, working parents) and your mind really struggles to find two hours in a block, where can you find a little more than fifteen minutes each day? That's all it takes! Schedule this time now like it's a VIP appointment and promise yourself that you're going to stick to it. This is going to be the most important healthy habit you're going to establish, so give it the commitment *you* deserve.

What you choose to do with these two hours is entirely up to you, but I'll tell you what you're not going to do: You're not to do anything that doesn't make your heart sing. You're not going to use these two hours to get a haircut if sitting in a salon bores you. You can, however, get a manicure if you feel pampered and relaxed after a manicure. These two hours aren't for playing catch-up on other commitments you've let fall; it's two hours to honor, love, and respect yourself. Pay attention to how you feel in this self-time. Anything relaxing or rejuvenating is in; anything boring or exhausting is out. If you want to spend your time hiking or watching trashy TV, go for it! It'll be different for everyone and it'll change over the weeks and months ahead, just so long as it feels good.

In my two hours this week, I will . . .

_____

_____

_____

_____

_____

YOUR DIVINE PHYSICAL SELF

Remember that awful exercise where I asked you to strip down in front of a mirror? You now get to do it again! Strip off and get your naked bod' in front of a mirror.

I feel (speak everything, only write down the not so positive) . . .

_____

_____

_____

_____

_____

Then verbalize the Intuitive Healing process, naming each uncomfortable emotion.

I allow myself to feel . . .
I give myself permission to feel . . .
I accept that I feel . . .

If this is your life's most challenging aspect, you'll most likely struggle to accept what you feel. Do your best to simply stay present with the emotion. Have you heard the saying, "What we resist, persists"? In order to have a body you love, you have to begin to accept your body. Just. As. It. Is. Still looking in the mirror, name one thing you like about your body. It could be your smile, your hair, or your little toe. Place your hand on that part of your body and say out loud why you like it, then write it down here:

_____

_____

_____

_____

_____

CONSCIOUS RELATIONSHIPS

Looking at your list from last week, name three people you have the most challenging relationships with (this can include someone you're grieving). In the week ahead, pay attention to how you feel when you spend time with/think about these people. Name the good and not so good. Then process the not so good through to acceptance. If this is your second time doing the journal, you can name new people or go deeper on the same relationships.

1. In my relationship with _____

I feel . . . (name everything out loud but write down only the unpleasant stuff)

_____

_____

_____

I allow myself to feel . . . (the uncomfortable feelings only)
I give myself permission to feel . . . (the uncomfortable feelings only)
I accept that I feel . . . (the uncomfortable feelings only)

2. In my relationship with _____

I feel . . . _____

_____

_____

_____

_____

I allow myself to feel . . .
I give myself permission to feel . . .
I accept that I feel . . .

3. In my relationship with _____

I feel . . . _____

_____

_____

_____

_____

I allow myself to feel . . .
I give myself permission to feel . . .
I accept that I feel . . .

Heads up: ANY justification for resisting acceptance is tricksy mind sabotage, blocking you from transforming internally.

CONSCIOUS CREATION

Last weekend you began thinking about your current employment and/or financial situation and wrote down how it makes you feel. Look back at this list. Now get more discerning and specific. For example, if being at work makes you feel awful, digging deeper, the feelings might stem from feeling disrespected, or your energy is being drained. If finances make you feel stressed, below that you might feel you're no good, or hopeless. What we're digging for here are the underlying insecurities or belief systems, the root of the problem, because these are what need to be transformed.

When I dig deeper into these feelings, I feel . . .

_____

_____

_____

_____

Process these deeper feelings/insecurities/beliefs into acceptance.

    I allow myself to feel . . .
    I give myself permission to feel . . .
    I accept that I feel . . .

Weekend Bonus Homework (for you self-help high achievers): Get outside, no matter what the weather, and spend some time in nature. You do know we are part of nature, not separate from it, yes? The simple act of getting out in nature and acknowledging this wondrous planet we are all part of, helps deepen our connection to who we really are.

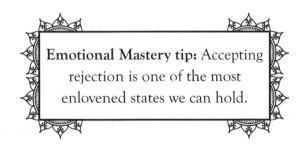

Emotional Mastery tip: Accepting rejection is one of the most enlovened states we can hold.

You are not being punished! You are being guided to the perfect experiences that increase your capacity to love.

Week 3 (Monday)

Time required: 5–10 minutes

On a scale of 1–10, where do you feel your life is at right now? _____

_____

Do you feel your life hasn't unfolded exactly the way you wished? Welcome to the club! You can either continue to resist where you are (which blocks you from moving forward), or you can start accepting exactly where you are and use it as a springboard for where you wish to be. Take a guess, which one is the more enlovened mindset?

Place a hand over your diaphragm and close your eyes. Take three deep breaths, bringing your awareness into the space behind your hand.

I feel (speak everything, write down only the unpleasant) . . .

_____

_____

_____

> I allow myself to feel (say this phrase out loud for each unpleasant emotion) . . .
> I give myself permission to feel (say this phrase out loud with each unpleasant emotion) . . .
> I accept that I feel (say this phrase out loud, working through each unpleasant emotion) . . .

Are you truly accepting all of what you feel? If not, why not? What does the mind say will happen? _____

_____

_____

Week 3 affirmation: "Where I am is the perfect springboard for where I wish to be." When I say this out loud three times, I feel . . .

_____

_____

_____

How you feel about this week's affirmation shows how accepting you are of your present life situation.

Week 3 (Tuesday)

Time required: about 5 minutes.

Place a hand over your diaphragm, close your eyes. Breathe into the space behind your hand. I feel . . .

_____
_____
_____
_____

Taking the uncomfortable emotions you've listed, say the following process out loud: "I allow myself to feel . . . I give myself permission to feel . . . I accept that I feel . . . "

Remember that kid in the playground no one wanted to play with? They're your uncomfortable emotions. It's time to grow up and start ~~playing~~ accepting them.

One thing I like about my body . . . _____

Week 3 affirmation: "Where I am is the perfect springboard for where I wish to be." When I say this out loud three times, I feel . . .

_____
_____
_____
_____

If the mind really resists this affirmation, process the resistance.

Notes & Ideas:

_____
_____
_____
_____
_____
_____
_____

Week 3 (Wednesday)

Time required: about 5 minutes.

Place a hand over your diaphragm, close your eyes. Breathe into the space behind your hands.

I feel . . .

_____

_____

_____

_____

Process the uncomfortable emotions, saying out loud: "I allow myself to feel . . . I give myself permission to feel . . . I accept that I feel . . . "

You can't deeply and powerfully transform emotional wounds (in the next Intuitive Healing steps) if you're not in authentic acceptance to begin with.

One thing I like about my body (a different thing from yesterday) . . . _____

Have you scheduled two hours for yourself this week? How does that feel?

_____

Week 3 affirmation: "Where I am is the perfect springboard for where I wish to be." When I say this out loud three times, I feel . . .

_____

_____

_____

_____

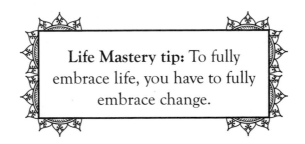

Life Mastery tip: To fully embrace life, you have to fully embrace change.

Week 3 (Thursday)

Time required: about 5 minutes.

Place a hand over your diaphragm, close your eyes. Breathe into the space behind your hand.

I feel . . .

_____

_____

_____

_____

Process the uncomfortable emotions, saying out loud: "I allow myself to feel . . . I give myself permission to feel . . . I accept that I feel . . . "

A big part of transforming old wounds into wisdom is to look for the gifts of knowing how it feels to experience these so called "negative" emotions. The gifts or wisdom I gained from feeling this way (write it down) . . .

_____

_____

_____

_____

One thing I like about my body (yes, a different thing from yesterday) . . .

_____

Week 3 affirmation: "Where I am is the perfect springboard for where I wish to be." When I say this out loud three times, I feel . . .

_____

_____

_____

_____

Week 3 (Friday)

Time required: about 5 minutes.

Place a hand over your diaphragm, close your eyes. Breathe into the space behind your hand. I feel . . .

_____

_____

_____

_____

Process the uncomfortable emotions, saying out loud: "I allow myself to feel . . . I give myself permission to feel . . . I accept that I feel . . . The gifts or wisdom I gained from feeling this way (write it down) . . . "

_____

_____

_____

_____

If you're struggling to find the gift of uncomfortable emotions, I've put a small guide at the end of the journal for the more common emotions. You're welcome!

One thing I like about my body (you know how this goes; a different thing each day) . . .

_____

Week 3 affirmation: "Where I am is the perfect springboard for where I wish to be." When I say this out loud three times, I feel . . .

_____

_____

_____

_____

Notes & Ideas:

_____

_____

_____

_____

WEEKEND WORDS OF WISDOM

It's a survival mechanism of the body to resist change. Around weeks 3, 6, and 12 of any new routine, sabotage will kick in, so be on the lookout for anything that prevents you from finding time to do this journal. If you can make it through these weeks, you'll begin to establish a healthy new pattern of connecting to who you authentically are.

If you're struggling to accept and find the gifts of uncomfortable emotions, are you more compassionate or understanding? Maybe less naïve? Pain is an incredibly healthy emotion, teaching us boundaries and helping us grow. Fear is another healthy emotion, which teaches caution and restraint. Knowing how it feels to be rejected leaves us more caring of others, and on a deeper level, there's the empowering realization that no one has the power to decide how we feel.

Story Time: Years ago, I went to an acupuncturist for neck pain I'd suffered for ages. I'd tried all sorts of physiotherapy and chiropractics, but nothing worked. As the acupuncturist put the needles in, he said the problem wasn't my neck but the jaw. He began massaging my jaw and suddenly it was like I'd taken opiates. I told the acupuncturist I knew the feeling because I'd had morphine when my wisdom teeth came out and this was exactly the same feeling. He then pressed his fingers right where my wisdom teeth would have been. I went from being high as a kite to bawling my eyes out. What else was going on when the wisdom teeth came out? I was suffering my first heartbreak. You see, the morphine had done its job all those years ago. It had stopped the pain, *all* my pain. By blocking me from feeling the heartbreak though, my body couldn't process and release it, so this trapped body pain had manifested in other ways.

Short-term, pharmaceuticals like painkillers and antidepressants can be helpful, long-term however, they stop the body being able to process and release pain.

P.S. I've never had neck problems again.

EVERY NEGATIVE EMOTION HAS SOMETHING POSITIVE TO TEACH

Emotions aren't good or bad, positive or negative; some are just more comfortable than others, and all offer opportunities for growth. Finding the gifts and wisdom behind our less comfortable emotions is the biggest challenge Intuitive Healing students initially face. Do you know we are not meant to be happy all the time? Think of times in your life when everything was super sweet, and then think about the most challenging times you've faced. When did you learn the most? Challenging emotions push us to grow. It's also through the contrast of life experiences that we fine tune what we really want. Your uncomfortable emotions are actually leading you, through discernment (i.e., "I know what I don't want"), to a more fulfilling and enriching life experience. If how you feel is incredibly painful, one immediate gift is the push to finally step up and do your inner work.

How are you doing with two self-hours each week? This process isn't complicated, but skipping days or exercises here and there makes it less effective. If you've been cheating, even by a few minutes, what is it that's causing you to not take time for yourself?

_____

No matter what it is, it's an excuse! An excuse to not honor and respect yourself.

How do you feel about taking two self-hours?

_____

_____

_____

_____

Process the uncomfortable feelings:

    I allow myself to feel . . .
    I give myself permission to feel . . .
    I accept that I feel . . .

The gift of feeling this is . . .

_____

_____

_____

_____

When people sabotage this exercise, it's usually because of guilt. Guilt is a form of manipulation, self-manipulation, and it's one of the most disempowering emotions we can feel. It's also the only emotion I won't work the Intuitive Healing process on. If you ever feel guilty, sit totally present in the feeling and see if you can dig into the underlying emotions or beliefs, such as "I'm a bad person" or "I won't be loved." Process the underlying emotions or beliefs, not the guilt. (If you can't figure what's underlying, you can start with "I feel manipulated.")

Tough Love Time: Guilt is used by powerless people, usually women, and often mothers. If you do something only because you've been guilted into it, you are allowing yourself to be manipulated. Not only that, the energy or intention behind everything we do is contained in our actions. If we act from manipulation we are spreading this most disempowering energy, like a virus, through our behavior. People who wield guilt also tend to martyr themselves, another hugely disempowering and manipulative emotion.

LIFELONG WISHES

If today were your last day on Earth, what do you wish you'd enjoyed, experienced, or accomplished that you haven't yet? It may seem a bit morbid to be thinking about death, but the surest way to not have any regrets is to remind ourselves that our time here is limited. A healthy way to look at death is the push to live each day to the fullest. Write down everything you wish you'd done if you were to pop your clogs today. Then go through the list and circle your top three—the three things you'd regret most. This list will include things that can't be accomplished overnight, like learning a second language or hiking Machu Picchu (these were two of mine, which I've now done . . . because I practice what I teach.)

This simple act of writing down your wishes sets universal forces into action. How cool is that!?

_____

_____

_____

_____

_____

_____

_____

_____

_____

YOUR DIVINE PHYSICAL SELF

It's that time of the week again! Time to strip down and look at your gorgeous physical self in the mirror. The more you do this exercise, the more comfortable you'll become.

When I look at this expression of life force energy in physical form, I feel . . ,

_____

_____

_____

_____

Circle the three most uncomfortable emotions above.

Can you remember how old you were when you first felt this way about your body?

_____

Why? What happened?

_____

_____

_____

_____

Was it your body's fault? (The answer to this is always no.)

Imagine your body as a child you've been rejecting your whole life. Now it's time to start loving that child, and we begin by accepting it—lumps, bumps, and flabby bits—just as it is!

Out loud, work through the Intuitive Healing process on the emotions you circled above while looking at your naked bod' in the mirror.

I allow myself to feel . . .
I give myself permission to feel . . .
I accept that I feel . . .

(Really push yourself into authentic acceptance)

The gift of feeling this way . . .

_____
_____
_____
_____

Heads up: Part of the ego's resistance to change means our inner critic (that nasty voice we all have in our head) will become particularly active. The self-empowering trick here is to hear what it says without listening to it. Don't try to block it out, as any resistance will just strengthen it. Notice what the critic tells you, but don't take it on board. It is not your truth! When the inner critic gets particularly loud, get excited, because some big self-empowering changes are afoot.

My inner critic often says (just writing it down is often enough to realize how ridiculous it is):

_____
_____
_____
_____

When I hear this voice, it sounds like (a person from your past, perhaps a parent or teacher) . . . _____

How evolved, as in, consciously enlightened, was this person? _____

Do you want this person to still have power over your life? _____

CONSCIOUS RELATIONSHIPS

Were you surprised by how badly some people can make you feel? Let's now shift this into a more empowering statement: "Up until now, I have ALLOWED people to make me feel this way." Yes, you have allowed them to make you feel bad. The question is: Why? What's in it for you? What are you getting out of this relationship to be allowing this? There has to be some payoff to allowing these people to treat you badly.

1. When I am with/think about . . . _____

I feel . . . _____

_____

_____

_____

_____

I allow this person to make me feel this way because . . . _____

_____

_____

_____

_____

2. When I am with/think about . . . _____

I feel . . . _____

_____

_____

_____

I allow this person to make me feel this way because . . . _____

_____

_____

_____

_____

3. When I am with/think about . . . _____

I feel . . . _____

_____

_____

_____

_____

I allow this person to make me feel this way because . . . _____

_____

_____

_____

_____

This exercise will require a degree of self-awareness, so dig deep and be honest. For example, "I allow my mother-in-law to be disrespectful because we're related/she's grandmother to my children," digging deeper you might get, "because I feel obligated" or "it keeps the peace." Or, "when I think about my deceased partner I feel loss," but digging deeper, "I am holding on to the loss because I feel it's the only connection I still have to them." If you struggle with this exercise, pay attention to how you feel as you spend time with these people or think about them during the week.

CONSCIOUS CREATION

When I'm at work/unemployed, or think about my finances, I feel (dig deep and name everything, no matter how challenging) . . .

_____

_____

_____

_____

Choose the three most uncomfortable emotions and work through them one at a time:

I allow myself to feel . . .
I give myself permission to feel . . .
I accept that I feel . . .

Sitting consciously in acceptance of the uncomfortable emotion, think of other times in your life when you also felt this way. Try to go back as far as you can (i.e., the youngest you can remember feeling this way).

What was happening? _____

_____

_____

_____

Who was involved? _____

_____

_____

_____

_____

Do you still want them or the situation to have power over your life? (This one was rhetorical.)

Do you see how the people or events that planted your early beliefs around self-worth or self-respect still have power over you? Life is too short not to be enjoying enriching and fulfilling work namely, a well-paying job you love, time to take back your power!

The gift of feeling this way (really push yourself with this) . . .

_____

_____

_____

_____

Even though this process might feel counterintuitive (it's not counterintuitive, it's actually counter-ego) each time you work through it you are reclaiming a bit of yourself, and a piece of your power back. When you "own" how someone or something made you feel, you make it yours. And once it's yours, you can do what you like with it. In this case, you own disempowering feelings/insecurities/beliefs through acceptance, then turn them into healthy self-esteem, self-worth, and self-respect, by finding the gifts and wisdom in the experience.

NOTE: We only ever process how we feel, not a statement of fact, e.g., "I feel I'm no good," never, "I am no good." This is because your emotions are simply perceptions of reality, which we can change. Contrary to what your mind may tell you, everything is just perception; actual reality is nonphysical vibrating fields of energy. Just ask a physicist!

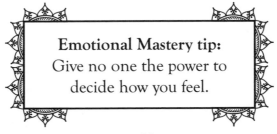

Emotional Mastery tip:
Give no one the power to
decide how you feel.

Self-love doesn't mean directing love at yourself, it's <u>allowing</u> love to flow through you. Every challenging life experience is an opportunity to carve your vessel deeper, increasing the capacity of this flow.

Week 4 (Monday)

On a scale of 1–10, how do you feel about where your life is at right now?

_____

Taking 5–10 minutes where you won't be interrupted, place a hand over your diaphragm and close your eyes. Breathe into the space behind your hand.

I feel . . .

_____
_____
_____
_____

Process the uncomfortable emotions, saying out loud:

    I allow myself to feel . . .
    I give myself permission to feel . . .
    I accept that I feel . . .

    The gifts or wisdom I gained from feeling this way . . .

_____
_____
_____
_____

Week 4 affirmation: "Every negative emotion has something positive to teach me." When I say this out loud three times, I feel . . .

_____
_____
_____
_____

Notes & Ideas:

_____
_____

Week 4 (Tuesday)

Time required: 5 minutes, give or take.

Place a hand over your diaphragm, close your eyes. Breathe into the space behind your hand. I feel . . .

_____

_____

_____

_____

Work the process for the uncomfortable emotions:

    I allow myself to feel . . .
    I give myself permission to feel . . .
    I accept that I feel . . .

    The gift of feeling this way is (write it down) . . .

_____

_____

_____

_____

If you're still struggling to think of the gifts, how are you a better person for having experienced this emotion?

One thing I like about my body: _____

Have you scheduled your two hours of self-time? _____

Week 4 affirmation: "Every negative emotion has something positive to teach me." When I say this out loud three times, I feel . . .

_____

_____

_____

_____

Week 4 (Wednesday)

Time required: 5 minutes, give or take.

Place a hand over your diaphragm, close your eyes. Breathe into the space behind your hand. I feel . . .

_____

_____

_____

_____

Out loud, work the process for any uncomfortable emotions:

I allow myself to feel . . .
I give myself permission to feel . . .
I accept that I feel . . .

The gift of feeling this way is (write down the gift) . . .

_____

_____

_____

_____

If you're really struggling with the gift, come join us cool kids at www.facebook/IntuitiveTherapy and ask any questions.

Name one positive thing about your body (a new thing from yesterday):

_____

Week 4 affirmation: "Every negative emotion has something positive to teach me." When I say this out loud three times, I feel . . .

_____

_____

_____

_____

Week 4 (Thursday)

Time required: 5 minutes, give or take.

Place a hand over your diaphragm, close your eyes. Breathe into the space behind your hand. I feel . . .

_____

_____

Out loud, work the process for any uncomfortable emotions:

> I allow myself to feel . . .
> I give myself permission to feel . . .
> I accept that I feel . . .

> The gift of feeling this way is . . .

_____

_____

_____

> I make peace with feeling . . .

If you are not at peace with how you feel, you are essentially at civil war with yourself. Time to wave the white flag!

One (new) thing my body does really well: _____

Week 4 affirmation: "Every negative emotion has something positive to teach me." When I say this out loud three times, I feel . . .

_____

_____

_____

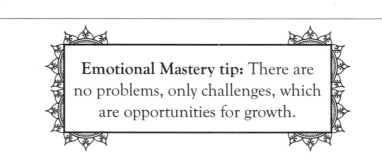

Emotional Mastery tip: There are no problems, only challenges, which are opportunities for growth.

Week 4 (Friday)

Time required: 5 minutes, give or take.

Place a hand over your diaphragm, close your eyes. Breathe into the space behind your hand. I feel . . .

_____

_____

Out loud, work the process for any uncomfortable emotions:

I allow myself to feel . . .
I give myself permission to feel . . .
I accept that I feel . . .

The gift of feeling this way is . . .

_____

_____

_____

_____

I make peace with feeling . . .

If you feel emotionally exhausted, it's because you are battling your emotions. Make peace and allow all that energy you were fighting to now work with you.

One (new) thing I like about my body: _____

Are you sticking to your two self-hours? If not, why not (and process any uncomfortable feelings)?

_____

_____

_____

Week 4 affirmation: "Every negative emotion has something positive to teach me." When I say this out loud three times, I feel . . .

_____

_____

_____

_____

WEEKEND WORDS OF WISDOM

Although I'm convinced sloths are one of the most enlightened animals on the planet, sitting around all day doing nothing isn't going to leave you satisfied. A common question I get asked in workshops is, "if I make peace with where I am, how will I get anything done?" The answer is: Inspired Action. This process isn't passive! We are life force energy in physical form, here to experience all the external physical world has to offer. All creation begins on the inside. If you take action from feeling not good enough, needing recognition, or have something to prove, then everything you do, everything you create, will have the underlying energy of insecurity in it. If you create from lack, then all your achievements will eventually leave you unfulfilled because the very essence of your creations are imbued with lack. If you don't heal and transform internally, no amount of external validation or achievement will ever be enough. And irrespective of your intentions, you will be spreading more unconsciousness in everything you do.

Up until now, most manifestation on the planet has been born of insecurity. This rise in global consciousness which you are part of, leads to a shift from insecure action to Inspired Action, and it's a wonderful thing to behold.

Story Time: One of the few structures (outside of art) I've stood in front of and felt Inspired Action at work is a 350-year-old mausoleum. "The teardrop on the cheek of time" was built as an expression of love, not of ego, victory, or defense. With over seven million visitors a year, I'm not the only one drawn to the love that is steeped in the Taj Mahal.

THE MOST IMPORTANT RELATIONSHIP YOU HAVE

How are you doing with scheduling and sticking to two hours each week for yourself? Do you need to get out your planner and move some things around? When you do take this time for yourself, how does it feel?

_____

_____

_____

_____

Process any uncomfortable emotions through to the gifts. Bask in the positive feelings; say to the universe, "more of this!"

Look at the three Lifelong Wishes you chose at the end of last week. What are the reasons (excuses!) you've told yourself as to why you've never accomplished these things? How do these excuses (i.e., lack of time or money) make you feel? Process these emotions through to the gifts/wisdom.

_____

_____

_____

_____

YOUR DIVINE PHYSICAL SELF

Yep, you guessed it! Time to strip down and look at that beautiful buck-naked body in the mirror again. How do you feel looking at yourself?

_____

_____

_____

_____

Process the uncomfortable emotions:

> I allow myself to feel . . .
> I give myself permission to feel . . .
> I accept that I feel . . .

If you really struggle with this aspect of your life, you are most likely looking at the physical manifestation of a childhood wound. Every time you look in the mirror and think something negative, you are allowing a painful past to continue to impact your present. You are allowing people and events to still have power over you. Time to take it back!

Digging deep into painful feelings, what false beliefs did you take on board about your body? (E.g., "I am unlovable," "there's something wrong with me," "I am too much.")

_____

_____

_____

_____

How has your body responded to these beliefs? (Hint: Most fat is a form of protection.)

_____

_____

_____

_____

When you look at how your body responded to what was going on in the past, can you be a bit more forgiving of where it currently is? Still standing naked in front of the mirror, work through every way you've been rejecting your body and find the gifts, then place your hands over that part of your body as you say "I thank my body for (example: stretch marks) because (example: they represent my beautiful kids) . . . "

For those of you who struggle with eating disorders, to truly heal this from within, pay attention to how you feel as you binge or purge. Process your feelings (usually self-hatred or loss of control) through to the end of the Intuitive Healing process (week 7). Do not be harsh on yourself. Your body is suffering enough without letting the inner critic get in there and add to the abuse. See this behavior for what it really is: the external, physical manifestation of internal, emotional wounds. These wounds aren't expressing themselves externally to punish you, they're trying to get your attention so they can be healed.

CONSCIOUS RELATIONSHIPS

The following process is for the disrespectful people in our lives. If you've been working on grief/loss, continue to process these feelings in the weekday meditation. If you get stuck, and the mind refuses to make peace, go back to last weekend's exercise and dig deeper into why you're holding on to the pain.

Do you know we teach people how to treat us? Bad behavior usually begins slowly, with one small thing which we can excuse, but then over time it escalates and often in such a way we don't even recognize the pattern until it's too late. You may have only been a child when your challenging relationships began—whatever the reason, don't beat yourself up for creating this monster. The good news is we can turn it around.

Look at the ~~answers~~ excuses you wrote down last week as to why you allow others to make you feel bad. We're now going to reword each excuse and bring to light the true cost of allowing this behavior.

I'll use the mother-in-law example from last week:

> I allow my mother-in-law to behave badly because . . . (internal reason) *it keeps the peace.*
> *Keeping the peace* . . . is more important than me speaking up for myself.
> *Peace* . . . is more valuable than my self-respect.
> I am worth less than . . . *peace with my mother-in-law.*
> I think I'm doing something good by . . . *keeping the peace* . . . but I am actually allowing myself to be hurt.
> Up until now I thought . . . *keeping the peace* . . . was a small price to pay, but really, I am allowing myself to be abused.

Let's call this behavior exactly what it is: abuse. It may not be physical, but emotional and psychological abuse are just as damaging. When we allow abuse, we inadvertently become advocates for abuse, which is how destructive energetic cycles are passed from generation to generation, family to family. If this aspect of your inner-transformation is your biggest challenge, be gentle on yourself and take your time with this exercise, fully exploring all the ways the disrespectful behavior of others is chipping away at your self-worth and self-esteem.

Heads up: Your mind might pipe in and say, "wise people choose their battles." If this behavior has gone on for a long time it's not a battle, it's a war. A war of attrition on your self-worth. This exercise will reveal to you the true cost of this war.

The Price I Pay for Others' Bad Behavior

_____

_____

_____

_____

_____

_____

_____

_____

_____

_____

CONSCIOUS CREATION

In a conscious world, what we do for a living, how we support ourselves, should be the physical expression of how our unique energy contributes to making the planet a better place. If you are hoping for any external validation through your position or title, your mind is missing the point and you will not be aligned with fulfilling work. We're now going to bring to the light of consciousness any false, ego-based notions around career or finances.

In my perfect career/job I will feel (dig deep here, naming both the noble and not so noble aspects) . . .

_____
_____
_____
_____
_____

If you struggle financially it's time to look at what money means to you. All money does is grease the wheels of trade, but for many of us, it represents something much greater. For some people money means power, safety, or being worthy. When I did this exercise (I practice what I teach) I thought money meant freedom.

If I made the "perfect"* amount of money for me, I would feel . . .

Be honest and name both the authentic and false/ego-based ideas.

_____
_____
_____
_____
_____

Circle the false ideas you hold around career or finances. This simple act of acknowledgment is a big first step in shifting our unhealthy beliefs.

Tough Love Time: Fame is a drug, a very addictive drug. If what you want in life is fame, you might as well be asking to be a drug addict, it'll be about as fulfilling and constructive. Dig deep into how you think fame will make you feel and process these emotions.

* It'll be a different amount for everyone.

Weekend Bonus Homework (for you gold star students): Get outside and look at the night sky. What phase is the moon at? Do you know when celestial events like eclipses or meteor showers are? Look them up and mark them in your calendar. Enjoying these events is a beautiful reminder of our connection to all things.

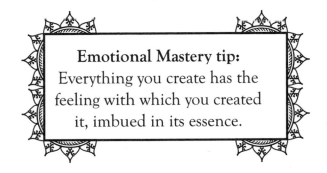

Emotional Mastery tip:
Everything you create has the feeling with which you created it, imbued in its essence.

Notes & Ideas:

_____

_____

_____

_____

_____

_____

_____

_____

_____

_____

_____

_____

_____

Fear of the future is a phobia, an irrational fear. No one can know how everything is going to turn out all the time, and if you did you'd get bored very quickly. Get excited by not knowing how things will turn out. See the unknown as an adventure.

Week 5 (Monday)

On a scale of 1–10, how do you feel about where your life is at right now?

_____

Taking 5–10 minutes where you won't be interrupted, place a hand over your diaphragm and close your eyes. Take three deep breaths, breathing into the space behind your hand.

I feel (write down the uncomfortable emotions) . . .

_____

_____

_____

Work the Intuitive Healing process for any uncomfortable emotions:

  I allow myself to feel . . .
  I give myself permission to feel . . .
  I accept that I feel . . .

  The gift of feeling this way is . . . (write it down)

_____

_____

_____

_____

  I make peace with feeling (speak the phrase out loud with each uncomfortable emotion) . . .

You should feel a sense of ease and grace when you make peace with how you feel.

One thing I like about my body (name a new thing each day) . . .

_____

Week 5 affirmation: "Every unpleasant experience in my life is an opportunity for growth." When I say this out loud three times, I feel . . .

_____

_____

_____

Week 5 (Tuesday)

Time required: 5-ish minutes

Place a hand over your diaphragm and close your eyes. Take three deep breaths, breathing into the space behind your hand. I feel (write down the uncomfortable emotions) . . .

_____

_____

_____

I allow myself to feel . . .
I give myself permission to feel . . .
I accept that I feel . . .

The gifts and wisdom of feeling this way are . . .

_____

_____

_____

_____

I make peace with feeling (speak the phrase out loud with each uncomfortable emotion). . .

You should be starting to feel yourself sinking "deeper" into your body as you continue to work this emotional transformation process.

One thing I enjoy about my fabulous body . . . _____

Week 5 affirmation: "Every unpleasant experience in my life is an opportunity for growth." When I say this out loud three times, I feel . . .

_____

_____

_____

_____

This can be a challenging affirmation. Remember not to judge or analyze how you feel, say it out loud and simply make a note of what it brings up for you, processing any challenging emotions.

Week 5 (Wednesday)

Time required: 5-ish minutes

Place a hand over your diaphragm and close your eyes. Take three deep breaths, breathing into the space behind your hand.

I feel (write down the uncomfortable emotions) . . .

_____

_____

_____

Process any uncomfortable emotions:

    I allow myself to feel . . .
    I give myself permission to feel . . .
    I accept that I feel . . .

    The gifts and wisdom of feeling this way are . . .

_____

_____

_____

_____

    I make peace with feeling (speak the phrase out loud with each uncomfortable emotion). . .

Take a few extra moments to sit in the relaxed state that is authentic inner peace!

One positive thing about this body of mine: _____

Week 5 affirmation: "Every unpleasant experience in my life is an opportunity for growth." When I say this out loud three times, I feel . . .

_____

_____

_____

_____

If there's an aspect of your past you are not at peace with, look at the big picture, asking how you're a wiser or more compassionate person because of the experience?

Week 5 (Thursday)

Time required: 5-ish minutes

Place a hand over your diaphragm and close your eyes. Take three deep breaths, breathing into the space behind your hand. I feel (write down the uncomfortable emotions) . . .

_____
_____
_____

Process the uncomfortable emotions:

    I allow myself to feel . . .
    I give myself permission to feel . . .
    I accept that I feel . . .

    The gifts and wisdom of feeling this way are . . .

_____
_____
_____

    I make peace with feeling (speak the phrase out loud with each uncomfortable emotion). . .
    I forgive myself for feeling (speak the phrase out loud with each uncomfortable emotion). . .

Forgiveness is not to say you've done anything wrong; it's about letting yourself off the hook for any old hurt you've been carrying around.

One glorious thing about my body: _____

Week 5 affirmation: "Every unpleasant experience in my life is an opportunity for growth." When I say this out loud three times, I feel . . .

_____
_____
_____

If you are holding on to anger or any form of resistance to a past event, it still has power over you. Own how you feel and process it, taking your power back!

Week 5 (Friday)

Time required: 5-ish minutes

Place your hands over your diaphragm and close your eyes. Take three deep breaths, breathing into the space behind your hands.

I feel (write down the uncomfortable emotions) . . .

_____

_____

Out loud, process the uncomfortable emotions:

    I allow myself to feel . . .
    I give myself permission to feel . . .
    I accept that I feel . . .
    The gifts and wisdom of feeling this way are . . .

_____

    I make peace with feeling . . .
    I forgive myself for feeling . . .

Forgiveness is a form of self-love. More on this with the weekend homework.

My body does this thing so well (remember, find a different thing each time) . . .

_____

Week 5 affirmation: "Every unpleasant experience in my life is an opportunity for growth." When I say this out loud three times, I feel . . .

_____

_____

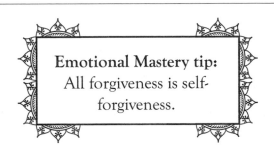

Emotional Mastery tip:
All forgiveness is self-forgiveness.

WEEKEND WORDS OF WISDOM

One of the most misunderstood self-help concepts is forgiveness. Forgiveness is never about another person, it's only ever about you. You don't forgive someone else for their behavior; you forgive yourself; not because you've necessarily done anything wrong but for the pain or anger you've been holding on to. If the mind gets caught on the word "forgive," how about apologizing? You apologize for how hard you have been on yourself. If you are holding yourself to a standard you wouldn't expect of others, then you're mistreating yourself. Forgiveness and apologizing are forms of authentic love. You should be able to feel yourself loving you as you work through this process.

YOUR MOST IMPORTANT RELATIONSHIP

If you're really struggling to let go of old pain and find peace, it's time to look at what part of your identity is coming from these uncomfortable emotions. The ego resists letting go of old slights and injuries because it has become attached and now sees itself as the wound rather than the radiant being of light you authentically are. No matter how traumatic the experience, don't let it define you. It is not who you are! By refusing to make peace you are limiting yourself and allowing a past experience to diminish you. Part of the current dialogue around sexual assault is the shift from victim to survivor. This is a tremendous self-empowering first step. Continuing to identify as any type of survivor however, holds you in battle or fight mode. To shift this into authentic love, see ALL experience as an opportunity to expand and evolve, increasing your capacity to self-love.

Up until now, I have allowed my ego to get identity from . . . (Include any so-called positive identity attachments, such as the college you attended, or awards and distinctions, because even these labels are limiting.)

_____

_____

_____

_____

Who would you be if you only felt gratitude and peace with your past?

_____

_____

_____

_____

How are you going with establishing a healthy habit of self-time? As I schedule and take two hours for myself each week, I feel . . .

_____
_____
_____
_____

Process any uncomfortable emotions through to forgiveness.

Looking at your Lifelong Wishes, choose the wish that seems most easily attainable. If the main excuse you'd told yourself didn't exist, what steps would you need to take to achieve this wish? Get very detailed, and write down every little thing necessary. If this is your second go through of the journal, continue moving towards your wishes or if you've already accomplished one of them (congratulations!) start on your next wish.

Lifelong Wish Action Plan:

_____
_____
_____
_____
_____
_____
_____
_____

YOUR DIVINE PHYSICAL SELF

You know what you need to do? Get your naked bod' in front of a mirror. Pay attention to any areas your eyes try to drift over.

I feel (write down the uncomfortable emotions) . . .

_____
_____
_____
_____

Out loud, work through the Intuitive Healing process on the above emotions:

    I allow myself to feel . . .
    I give myself permission to feel . . .
    I accept that I feel . . .

The gifts and wisdom of feeling this way are . . .
I make peace with feeling . . .
I forgive/apologize to myself for . . .

In order to see long-lasting results, we have to change from the inside before we take action on the outside. You've spent the past five weeks transforming your internal relationship with your body, and now it's time to take some external action. Yeah! Being realistic, what would you like to see when you look in the mirror? Keep in mind not even supermodels like everything they see.

_____

_____

_____

_____

How would you feel about your body if you achieved the above? Initially you might think it will be overwhelmingly positive to have a body you feel proud of, but if you've struggled with this aspect of your life, chances are there are some uncomfortable emotions lurking below the surface. If you had the "perfect" body for you, are you afraid of being seen? Getting unwanted attention? Or, if you fixed this, then you might have to look at what's *really* wrong with your life?

_____

_____

_____

_____

Process any uncomfortable emotions through to forgiveness.

For those of you who want to lose weight or really get in shape, the best way to do this is through a structured, professional program. Beware the sabotaging mind that tells you to do a little here and there. If you want a big shift in results (and don't want to be in the same place five years from now), a professional program is the only place to start. The good news is, because you've done your internal work, you will now vibrationally match the perfect program for you. If you've done a program previously and it worked for a while before you fell back to old habits, don't be disheartened. This time is different because of the inner-work you've been doing. In the past few weeks you have begun to fundamentally change the way you relate to your body, and this will be reflected in maintaining your health and fitness. In the week ahead, start researching diet/exercise programs and be ready to go by next weekend.

Diet or exercise plans that honor my divine physical being:

_____

_____

_____

_____

_____

_____

Heads up: Some people spend more on their cars (and are prouder) than they do on their own wonder of engineering!

CONSCIOUS RELATIONSHIPS

If you haven't done so in your weekday meditation, process any feelings brought up by unhealthy relationships through to forgiveness. Remember you are actually forgiving yourself, not the other person. Now that you understand the true cost of allowing others to treat you badly, we're going to look at establishing healthy new boundaries. If you've tried to stand up for yourself in the past but it didn't work, or eventually the old behavior reasserted itself, this time it will be different because you're now making changes from the inside out.

Heads up:

1. You're going to have to reinforce new boundaries repeatedly.
2. The other person will push back against these changes.
3. It will take energy, BUT it will be worth it!

Using our mother-in-law example from last week (by the way, I don't have a mother-in-law, so this isn't some underhanded swipe.)

> In my relationship with . . . *my mother-in-law.*
> I wish these things were different . . . *that I was respected/considered/listened to.*
> How would this play out, what exactly would this look like? *She wouldn't turn up unannounced/she wouldn't call daily/we wouldn't always have to go to her house.*
> I can establish a healthy boundary and start practicing self-respect today by . . . *telling her it's not appropriate to turn up unannounced/not answering the phone every time she calls/organizing for her to come to our place.*

1. In my relationship with . . . _____

I wish these things were different . . . _____

How would this play out, what exactly would this look like? _____

_____

_____

_____

_____

I can establish a healthy boundary and start practicing self-respect today by:

_____

_____

_____

_____

2. In my relationship with . . . _____

I wish these things were different . . . _____

How would this play out, what exactly would this look like? _____

_____

_____

_____

_____

I can establish a healthy boundary and start practicing self-respect today by:

_____

_____

_____

_____

3. In my relationship with . . . _____

I wish these things were different . . . _____

How would this play out, what exactly would this look like exactly? _____

_____

_____

_____

_____

I can establish a healthy boundary and start practicing self-respect today by:

_____

_____

_____

_____

If the thought of taking action scares you, look back at last week's "price" of allowing this behavior. Is the price of the action worth more than the price you are already paying? Unlikely.

Tough Love Time: If your mind is telling you your situation is unique and there's nothing you can do, then you're being a victim. If you won't help yourself, it doesn't matter how many self-help books you read or how much therapy you attend, your situation will never change.

CONSCIOUS CREATION

In his famous poem "If," Rudyard Kipling calls triumph and disaster impostors. In much the same way, success and failure are illusions. Our false belief around success centers on the notion that once we achieve something external (a dollar amount, a title, etc.), then we will feel happy/fulfilled/complete. What does success mean to you?

If I were successful in career and/or finances, I would feel . . . (name both the authentic and the false, ego-based ideas.)

_____

_____

_____

_____

Take whatever false ideas this uncovers, e.g., "I will feel I have arrived/belong/good enough," and rewrite this by naming the underlying insecurity, e.g., "I feel . . . lost/I don't belong/not good enough." Then process the insecurity through to self-forgiveness.

_____

_____

_____

_____

Once you see through the illusion of success, you'll also see through the BS of failure. All failure means is that the external world hasn't lined up the way our mind (read: ego) thought it should. It says nothing about who we are as a person. Simply put, failure is the mind using the lack of some external thing (money, a job title, a loving partner, having a child) as an excuse to hold you in a self-abusing pattern. Everyone has suffered setbacks in life; it's what we do with them that separates the consciously evolved from the mind/ego-trapped person. Accepting and then surrendering (the final Intuitive Healing step) to feeling like a failure will internally align you with the wisdom of authentic "inner" success.

Remember, we only ever process how we feel, never a statement of fact (i.e., never "I am a failure"; only "I feel like a failure"). There is a fundamental difference in this simple semantic shift. Who you are (the "I am") is far greater than the mind. How you feel is simply how we experience and interpret this physical time-space reality. Shifting how you feel changes not only your perception but also your relationship with the much bigger "I am," bringing you into alignment with who you really are.

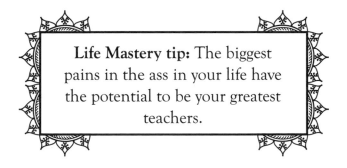

Life Mastery tip: The biggest pains in the ass in your life have the potential to be your greatest teachers.

Surrender is similar to an orgasm: really hard to explain to someone who hasn't felt it, but you just know when you have. And yes, surrender will feel that good.

Week 6 (Monday)

Heads up: In the next week or two, sabotage will usually try to derail your progress. Hang in there!

On a scale of 1–10, how do you feel about where your life is at right now? _____

Taking a few minutes where you won't be interrupted, place a hand over your diaphragm and close your eyes. Take three deep breaths, breathing into the space behind your hand.

I feel . . .

_____
_____
_____
_____

Out loud, process the uncomfortable emotions:

I allow myself to feel . . .
I give myself permission to feel . . .
I accept that I feel . . .
The gifts and wisdom of feeling this way are . . .
I make peace with feeling . . .
I forgive/apologize to myself for feeling . . .

My body does this thing really well (something new each time) . . . _____
_____

Any research you need to do on health / fitness programs? _____

Week 6 affirmation: look in a mirror and say "I'm so sorry for the times I've been hard on you; you've done the best you can. I love you." You can improvise a little with this affirmation. Use whatever words you need to hear that let yourself off the hook for any old wounds or resentments you've been holding on to. How does this make you feel?

_____
_____
_____
_____

Week 6 (Tuesday)

Time required: 5 or so minutes.

Place a hand over your diaphragm and close your eyes. Take three deep breaths, breathing into the space behind your hand.

I feel . . .

_____

_____

_____

_____

Out loud, process any uncomfortable emotions:

    I allow myself to feel . . .
    I give myself permission to feel . . .
    I accept that I feel . . .
    The gifts and wisdom of feeling this way are . . .
    I make peace with feeling . . .
    I forgive/apologize to myself for feeling . . .

My body is fabulous because . . . _____

Any more research you can add to your lifelong wish list? _____

_____

Week 6 affirmation: look in a mirror and say some variation of "I'm so sorry for the times I've been hard on you; you've done the best you can. I love you." When I look in the mirror and say this, I feel . . .

_____

_____

_____

_____

Notes & Ideas:

_____

_____

_____

Week 6 (Wednesday)

Time required: 5 or so minutes.

Place a hand over your diaphragm and close your eyes. Take three deep breaths, breathing into the space behind your hand.

I feel . . .

_____

_____

_____

_____

Out loud, process the uncomfortable emotions:

I allow myself to feel . . .
I give myself permission to feel . . .
I accept that I feel . . .
The gifts and wisdom of feeling this way are . . .
I make peace with feeling . . .
I forgive/apologize to myself for feeling . . .

The building block nature of this transformation process means everything won't fall into place if you haven't done all your homework. Get up to speed if there's any catching up you need to do.

By now you should have a really detailed plan for achieving one of your Lifelong Wishes. Yes, you should!

Week 6 affirmation: look in a mirror and say some variation of "I'm so sorry for the times I've been hard on you; you've done the best you can. I love you." When I look in the mirror and say this, I feel . . .

_____

_____

_____

_____

Week 6 (Thursday)

Time required: 5 or so minutes.

Place a hand over your diaphragm and close your eyes. Take three deep breaths, breathing into the space behind your hand. I feel . . .

_____

_____

_____

_____

Out loud, process the uncomfortable emotions:

> I allow myself to feel . . .
> I give myself permission to feel . . .
> I accept that I feel . . .
> The gifts and wisdom of feeling this way are . . .
> I make peace with feeling . . .
> I forgive/apologize to myself for feeling . . .

Surrender is the final step on this road to emotional mastery and one of the most enlovened states we can hold. Say out loud, "I surrender to feeling (the uncomfortable emotions)." How does this feel?

If Health & Fitness are one of your great challenges, finish up researching diet/exercise plans and get all your ducks in a row. This weekend, be ready to roll!

Week 6 affirmation: look in a mirror and say some variation of "I'm so sorry for the times I've been hard on you; you've done the best you can. I love you." When I look in the mirror and say this, I feel . . .

_____

_____

_____

_____

Notes & Ideas:

_____

_____

Week 6 (Friday)

Time required: 5 or so minutes.

Place a hand over your diaphragm and close your eyes. Take three deep breaths, breathing into the space behind your hand. I feel . . .

_____

_____

_____

_____

Out loud, process the uncomfortable emotions:

    I allow myself to feel . . .
    I give myself permission to feel . . .
    I accept that I feel . . .
    The gifts and wisdom of feeling this way are . . .
    I make peace with feeling . . .
    I forgive/apologize to myself for feeling . . .
    I surrender to feeling . . .

Surrender is not defeat and it is not passive. It is complete nonresistance to the present moment.

Week 6 affirmation: look in a mirror and say some variation of "I'm so sorry for the times I've been hard on you; you've done the best you can. I love you." When I look in the mirror and say this, I feel . . .

_____

_____

_____

_____

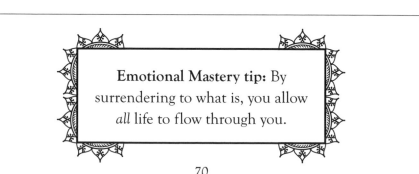

Emotional Mastery tip: By surrendering to what is, you allow *all* life to flow through you.

WEEKEND WORDS OF WISDOM

Are you noticing a shift in how you relate to yourself and the external world? Are you being a bit more forgiving and loving of yourself? (These were rhetorical questions.)

We're now up to the big boss in your healing journey: SURRENDER. A common misconception is that surrender is passive when, in fact, it's active. Surrender is not resignation, nor does it mean giving your power away. Surrender is the complete letting go of any resistance to "what is," bringing you into total alignment with the present moment. It's okay if your mind initially resists surrender. People often feel vulnerable when they first surrender. Know this: vulnerability is true strength! Vulnerability is to stand wholly in who you are, knowing that if others don't get you, it will be like water off a duck's back. You hold your own internal alignment, loving you just as you are . . . and by extension, genuinely loving others just as they are. It's a flexible strength, a flowing strength. Authentic self-love means no exhausting shields or barriers are necessary, but any barbs and arrows won't find their mark either.

This ultimate self-empowering concept of surrender will come to you more through practice than theory as you continue to work through the exercises and meditations in different areas of your life.

INSPIRED ACTION

When we take action from a place of surrender, known as *inspired action*, we see some very powerful results. When you embrace all of who you authentically are, you don't create to cover a lack, you create to expand your joy. All action and creation extends the love you feel within, not for anyone or any outcome, but purely for the pleasure of it. You create because it feels so damn good to create! When you are inspired to take action, you are like a conductor channeling life force energy, and it's one of the most deeply satisfying feelings we can experience. The blissful natural high you get is what life force energy feels like in its unmanifested form. With Inspired Action, you are experiencing yourself as Source energy.

Inspired Action cannot be forced; it's an effortless grace which only arrives when you are in surrender. Although Inspired Action is effortless, there can still be commitment and dedication, but it is never pushed. It does not exhaust or deplete; instead it enlivens and enriches, feeding your soul. You can feel the difference between insecure action and Inspired Action. Inspired Action has a magnetic, captivating quality. Mesmerizing works of art, like the statue of *David*, are your authentic self recognizing life force energy, a.k.a. love, and basking in the vibration of it. Music that lifts and transports you to another place was created from this place of aligned inspiration. Any performance that feels hypnotic or spellbinding is Inspired Action at work. This journal was also created from Inspired Action.

You create the right environment for creativity and inspiration through acceptance and surrender. Being at total peace with who you are and where you are also means allowing creative seeds to arrive unformed. Giving them time to germinate without judgment or impatience. The downtime is just as important as the doing time. Be at peace with tinkering about purely for the pleasure of tinkering about, knowing that when inspiration shows up, you'll be ready. Divine timing is another form of Inspired Action. There is an ease and grace when we feel galvanized to act from inner guidance. Being in the right place at the right time only happens when the mind steps aside and we surrender to the present moment.

Ready for some fun? It's time to start actioning one of your Lifelong Wishes. You've done your research (because you did your homework) and now it's time for some Inspired Action. Look at the steps you detailed in last week's homework. What can you action right now? Don't get overwhelmed if it's a huge list that will take months or years to implement. Look at the first step. Do it! Every week you're going to do one thing, no matter how big or small, that moves you towards achieving this goal. The time you devote to your Lifelong Wishes can count toward your two self-hours each week.

Heads up: The energy of asking for something is *very* different from the energy of receiving it. To switch from asking mode to receiving mode, stop longing for this lifelong wish and instead see it is a given. Act with a sense of certainty that achieving your wish will happen.

Inspired Action I plan to take towards a lifelong wish this week:

_____

_____

_____

_____

_____

_____

_____

_____

YOUR DIVINE PHYSICAL SELF

If this area of your life is one you really struggle with, you should have spent the past week researching different diet/exercise programs, and now it's time to choose one that *feels* right and begin today!

For as many Intuitive Healing students who feel they need to start dieting or exercise, there are those who are abusing their bodies in another way. They diet or exercise too much. If you are always on some sort of diet or do high-impact exercise five (or more) times a week, then you are abusing your divine physical self. The body needs rest. A break from a restrictive diet and excessive exercise will allow the body to find its own healthy balance. If you are one of these people (you know who you are!), your homework in the week ahead is to ease up on the diet or only do high impact exercise four times a week and process what emotions this brings up for you. To be clear, I'm not talking about pigging out on junk food or never exercising again—true health is balance, not punishing discipline.

Heads up: Even if something is considered healthy, like working out, if you're doing it to an extreme it's still damaging behavior.

Stand naked in front of a mirror, and say out loud: (You didn't think we'd skip this fabulous exercise, did you?)

I feel . . .
I allow myself to feel . . .
I give myself permission to feel . . .
I accept that I feel . . .
The gifts and wisdom of feeling this way are . . .
I make peace with feeling . . .
I forgive/apologize to myself for feeling . . .
I surrender to feeling . . .

In the end of week 4 homework, you paid attention to how you'd been rejecting one particular part of your body. Another way of saying this is how you've been rejecting an aspect of the divine in physical form. By beating yourself up for one part of your physique, you're disrespecting and dishonoring the incredible feat of engineering that you inhabit. Whether it's cellulite, a big nose, ugly feet, or fat thighs, see this most challenging aspect of your physical self as the perfect opportunity to increase your capacity to (self-) love.

Up until now, the biggest challenge I've had with my body has been . . .

_____

_____

_____

_____

Work the Intuitive Healing process through to surrender on this most challenging aspect. If you still have difficulty finding the gifts or wisdom of one physical part of yourself, know that it has been teaching you unconditional love. Pretty cool, huh?

Tough Love Time: Those who complain most about their bodies are usually the ones who do the least to help their bodies. Starting today, you will NO LONGER complain about any aspect of your physical self! Did you get that? If you go to complain, catch yourself, and then work the Intuitive Healing process on the underlying feelings.

CONSCIOUS RELATIONSHIPS

As you interact with your most challenging people, in your head work the Intuitive Healing process through to surrender. If you get too caught up in the moment while you're with these people, take an "energetic break" by physically removing yourself, e.g., step outside or into the bathroom, whatever you can do to disconnect from the dynamic, then work the process. Wise person that you now are, you know your relationships with other people are just a reflection of your relationship with yourself. The more resistance these people put up to your new healthy boundaries, the more entrenched your own disempowering beliefs, so use their resistance to dig deeper into your own issues around self-worth . . . and process them.

If one of your relationships seems like it will never change no matter what you do, don't give up! There is Inspired Action you can take around all relationships, but first you have to surrender to where the relationship is right now. In the week ahead, surrender, then allow Inspired Action to guide you into putting up all sorts of creative, possibly even sneaky*, healthy boundaries.

If you've seen some initial success with your external relationships, you're going to have to keep it up. You've most likely shifted a very old dynamic, and even if the other person seems to have changed, they will try to fall back into the old pattern if you let them. Don't get frustrated with your progress if/when this happens, simply see it as an opportunity to reaffirm this healthy new relationship with yourself. If you have any repeat offenders, it might be the universe telling you to cut them out of your life or, at the least, reassign them from your inner to your outer circle (more on this next week). Establishing healthy boundaries is like learning to walk; you're going to fall on your butt a few times. The important thing is to learn from each experience and think about how you'd do it differently if/when it happens again.

1. Up until now in my relationship with _____

I allowed this unhealthy behavior . . . _____

Inspired Action I can take to reaffirm healthy new boundaries . . . _____

_____

_____

_____

_____

2. Up until now in my relationship with _____

I allowed this unhealthy behavior . . . _____

Inspired Action I can take to reaffirm healthy new boundaries . . . _____

_____

_____

_____

_____

3. Up until now in my relationship with _____

I allowed this unhealthy behavior . . . _____

Inspired Action I can take to reaffirm healthy new boundaries . . .

_____

_____

_____

_____

* I see no problem with a little white lie to help us establish healthy new boundaries.

CONSCIOUS CREATION

The most common underlying insecurity people harbor around career or finances is one of powerlessness. What they do for a living or how much they get paid feels outside their control. Time to turn this around! You may not be able to control the externals, but you *can* decide the internals, that is how you feel about it.

Empowerment is an internal state. If you need the external world to be a certain way before you feel empowered, then your mind has mistaken power for control. Control is a false ego belief. You have no control over anything in the external world in the long run. Read that last sentence again. Does your mind accept or resist that statement? The only thing you have a say in, is how you feel about external events, and this is *mastery*, not control.

Processing powerlessness can be very challenging; however, the gifts and wisdom of allowing yourself to feel powerless are huge. When you authentically surrender to feeling powerlessness over external conditions, you'll sense a subtle but important internal shift take place. As you let go of external attachment, you will reconnect internally with your authentic-empowered-self.

Whatever your deepest insecurity around career/finances, it's time to transform it:

When I think about my career and/or finances, I feel . . . _____

_____

_____

_____

_____

Dig deep! The underlying feelings/insecurities/unhealthy beliefs are . . . _____

_____

_____

_____

_____

    I allow myself to feel . . .
    I give myself permission to feel . . .
    I accept that I feel . . .

The gifts and wisdom of feeling this way are (really go to town with this step) . . .

_____

_____

_____

_____

_____

I make peace with feeling . . .
I forgive/apologize to myself for feeling . . .
I surrender to feeling . . .

> **Life Mastery tip:** True self-empowerment is a deep inner knowing that whatever life throws your way, you will be okay.

Notes & Ideas:

_____

_____

_____

_____

_____

_____

_____

_____

_____

_____

_____

Say the word "control," and feel the restrictive, exhausting energy of it. Now say "mastery"—can you feel the ease and flow?

Week 7 (Monday)

On a scale of 1–10, how do you feel about where your life is at right now? _____

Taking 5–10 minutes where you won't be interrupted, place a hand over your diaphragm and close your eyes. Take three deep breaths, breathing into the space behind your hand. I feel . . .

_____

_____

_____

_____

Out loud, process the uncomfortable emotions:

> I allow myself to feel . . .
> I give myself permission to feel . . .
> I accept that I feel . . .
> The gifts and wisdom of feeling this way are . . .
> I make peace with feeling . . .
> I forgive/apologize to myself for feeling . . .
> I surrender to feeling . . .

Remember, no BS'ing yourself, really own what you feel and stay present as you work this process. Authentic surrender is a state of grace; if you feel anything else, you're in resistance.

Name two positive things about your body: _____

_____

Have you ever looked at a baby's body and thought how friggin' cute they are? All flabby arms and wobbly legs, but still totally adorable. That is the same type of adoration you want to be bringing to your own wonder of engineering.

Week 7 affirmation: "I am capable and I back myself. No matter what life brings, I will be okay." When I say this out loud three times, I feel . . .

_____

_____

_____

_____

Week 7 (Tuesday)

Time required: whatever feels self-respecting.

Place a hand over your diaphragm and close your eyes. Take three deep breaths, breathing into the space behind your hand. I feel . . .

_____

_____

_____

_____

Out loud, process the uncomfortable emotions:

> I allow myself to feel . . .
> I give myself permission to feel . . .
> I accept that I feel . . .
> The gifts and wisdom of feeling this way are . . .
> I make peace with feeling . . .
> I forgive/apologize to myself for feeling . . .
> I surrender to feeling . . .

Authentic surrender is total alignment with who you really are. It feels really good, otherwise, you're in resistance.

Three positive things about my body (different from yesterday): _____

_____

Steps I take this week to action a Lifelong Wish: _____

_____

How does it feel when you take these steps? _____

_____

Week 7 affirmation: "I am capable and I back myself. No matter what life brings, I will be okay." When I say this out loud three times, I feel . . .

_____

_____

_____

_____

Week 7 (Wednesday)

Time required: whatever feels self-respecting.

Place a hand over your diaphragm and close your eyes. Take three deep breaths, breathing into the space behind your hand. I feel . . .

_____

_____

_____

_____

Out loud, process the uncomfortable emotions:

> I allow myself to feel . . .
> I give myself permission to feel . . .
> I accept that I feel . . .
> The gifts and wisdom of feeling this way are . . .
> I make peace with feeling . . .
> I forgive/apologize to myself for feeling . . .
> I surrender to feeling . . .

If you're resisting surrender, what is the mind saying? _____

Four fabulous things my body does . . . _____

_____

_____

_____

You hear so much about gratitude in the spiritual world that it's become a bit of a turnoff. Like, "one more effing thing I have to do!" Much of this process focuses on what isn't working (because that's what needs to change), so daily gratitude is a small "thank you" to the universe for the good stuff.

Today, I am grateful for . . . _____

Week 7 affirmation: "I am capable and I back myself. No matter what life brings, I will be okay." When I say this out loud three times, I feel . . .

_____

_____

_____

Week 7 (Thursday)

Time required: whatever feels self-respecting.

Place a hand over your diaphragm and close your eyes. Take three deep breaths, breathing into the space behind your hand. I feel . . .

_____

_____

_____

_____

Out loud, process the uncomfortable emotions:

> I allow myself to feel . . .
> I give myself permission to feel . . .
> I accept that I feel . . .
> The gifts and wisdom of feeling this way are . . .
> I make peace with feeling . . .
> I forgive/apologize to myself for feeling . . .
> I surrender to feeling . . .

Authentic surrender is a state of liberation; liberation from resistance.

Five amazing things about my body: _____

_____

_____

_____

Appreciation for what we already have powerfully aligns us with more things to be grateful for. Tell me something amazing about this incredible life journey you're on?

_____

_____

Week 7 affirmation: "I am capable and I back myself. No matter what life brings, I will be okay." When I say this out loud three times, I feel . . .

_____

_____

_____

Week 7 (Friday)

Time required: whatever feels self-respecting.

Place a hand over your diaphragm and close your eyes. Take three deep breaths, breathing into the space behind your hand. I feel . . .

_____

_____

_____

_____

Out loud, process the uncomfortable emotions:

> I allow myself to feel . . .
> I give myself permission to feel . . .
> I accept that I feel . . .
> The gifts and wisdom of feeling this way are . . .
> I make peace with feeling . . .
> I forgive/apologize to myself for feeling . . .
> I surrender to feeling . . .

Authentic surrender is true freedom. If you want to feel free get into surrender.

Six sexy things about my body: _____

_____

_____

All creation begins on the inside, and gratitude is no different. Send gratitude to yourself for a challenge you've overcome . . . _____

Week 7 affirmation: "I am capable and I back myself. No matter what life brings, I will be okay." When I say this out loud three times, I feel . . .

_____

_____

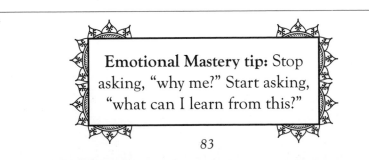

Emotional Mastery tip: Stop asking, "why me?" Start asking, "what can I learn from this?"

WEEKEND WORDS OF WISDOM

The easiest way to make the shift from disempowerment to empowerment, is to stop asking "why me?" It doesn't matter how old you were, or how painful the event, changing your mindset to "what can I learn from this?" or, "how am I a better person?" is how we grow from even the toughest of situations. Take the gifts from your most challenging experiences and send gratitude to yourself for the wisdom and growth they have afforded you. This simple mindset switch internally aligns us with becoming the lovers we authentically are.

YOUR MOST IMPORTANT RELATIONSHIP

Find a space where you won't be disturbed. Get comfortable and light a white candle. Think about the area of your life that causes you the most pain. Dig deep and get really specific with how you feel:

_____

_____

_____

_____

Stay present in the pain and say out loud, "show me where this began." In your mind's eye, start going back through your life, like you are flicking through a catalog. Allow your mind's eye to take you younger and younger as you sit in your discomfort. The images in your head will eventually stop on a certain point in your life. Don't judge or dismiss what you're seeing, even if it seems to have no connection to your current pain. Still sitting in the pain, go into the place where your mind's eye took you and let your imagination play out a scene from your past. Whether a specific event or just a certain time in your life, be totally present and *feel* everything you felt then.

Once the scene has played through, say to your younger self, "I am sorry you had to go through that. And I'm really sorry I wasn't there to take care of you. Can you forgive me?" What response does younger you give?

_____

_____

_____

_____

You're now going to play through the entire scene again but this time, you of today is going to be there with your younger self, either holding their hand or hugging them (if they'll let you.) Don't diminish how younger you feels or interprets the events, just let them know you are there with them.

Once the scene has played through for the second time, tell younger you that you are now here to take care of things and you will *never* leave them again. Whatever loving words your younger self needs to hear, speak them (out loud) now. When you've said all that needs to be said, ask younger you, "How has this experience made me a better person?" Pay attention to what younger you says, even if it doesn't seem relevant. You might even get images of other times in your life where you understood something or behaved in a certain way because of this initial experience. Write it all down:

_____

_____

_____

_____

_____

Then say, "thank you for these gifts, I am indeed a wiser person." (Be genuinely grateful as you speak to your younger self, as they may have gone through hell to give you this gift.) In the weeks and months ahead, if you feel any old residual fear or pain from this past experience, hold the discomfort and consciously send gratitude to that part of yourself. Now ask your younger self, "what do you need to heal and make peace?" They might ask for a specific thing or wish to replay events again in a self-empowering way. Whatever it is, write down what they needed:

_____

_____

_____

Your homework is to give younger you what they need in order to heal and let go. It might seem childish or small, but listening to and honoring all of yourself is one of the foundations of self-love. When I did this process, younger me asked for a brand-new pink dress. Being a bit of a tomboy, I grew up wearing my older brothers' hand-me-downs, and my little girl felt forgotten. I went out and bought a pink cotton dress, not the most fashionable thing for a thirty-something-year-old woman, but my little girl was overjoyed. What our oldest, deepest wounds need to heal will always be respectful and empowering. If they are asking for something destructive or harmful, process how this feels, then ask them again.

YOUR DIVINE PHYSICAL SELF

If this aspect of self-love is your biggest challenge, as you begin to set new healthy habits for diet or exercise, any sabotaging beliefs will begin to surface. To put it bluntly, losing weight or hitting the gym (or stopping these if you do it too much) can bring up a shed-load of self-loathing and doubt. When we make big external shifts like dieting or exercise, we trigger any unaligned internal energy. In the weeks ahead, old behavior that would have sabotaged you in the past will be making itself known. Stay on top of it by writing down any undermining thing that comes up, then digging deep into the underlying emotions and working through the Intuitive Healing process. Remember, what you're doing here is establishing a new pattern of health and fitness, so how you chose to navigate any setbacks speaks volumes for where you are regarding self-respect and self-esteem.

If you forget a day or for whatever reason fall off the bandwagon with regard to your health and fitness, don't beat yourself up; just start again. See whatever sabotage pops up as an opportunity for growth. Be mindful of how clever and creative sabotage can be. Don't like your new gym? Just found out you have a health issue that'll conflict with your diet? See all of this for what it is: sabotage! Another common form of sabotage will be for the body to get sick or injured. In the weeks ahead, if you find you have to miss a day due to circumstances that seem totally outside of your control (actually, you are that powerful) try to find an alternative that still keeps you moving forward with your new diet/exercise plan. Whatever comes up, make the necessary adjustments and push on through.

How I brilliantly overcame some sneaky sabotage that tried to derail my new health and fitness program:

_____

_____

_____

_____

For those who are working on cutting back on either dieting or exercising, it will usually trigger control issues. Take a look at what other areas of your life feel out of control and where you are overcompensating through how you treat your body. If this is one of your biggest challenges, do the previous exercise of going back through time with your younger self, to look at where it all began. When you have a healthy connection with your physical body (what you've been working on for the past seven weeks), it will tell you what it needs. And when you diet/exercise from this self-respecting place, your body will find its "perfect" weight and shape, and injuries become a thing of the past.

Tough Love Time: If you're one of those people who used to complain about their body, be wary of any victim identity attachment to being overweight, sick, or injured.

Wait? What! You thought we'd skip your new bestie, the mirror? Get that gorgeous naked bod' in front of a mirror and process any uncomfortable emotions through to surrender. Then look at your body and say, "I chose you." Because you did. Yes, you did! You knew the general shape and size, the color of your hair and skin, if you are conventionally attractive or not, and the particular challenges this body would bring. And you chose it. Depending on how far you've come with this aspect of self-love, you'll either say "I chose you" and smile, or you'll think, hell no! If you're in the latter group, process how saying "I chose you" makes you feel. If you're in the former group, say "and I'd choose you again in a heartbeat." Play around with whatever words feel right as you reintroduce yourself to this numinous (fabulous word, not a typo) being standing in front of you. This once in ALL time body, that will never, ever exist again, who you *chose* to go on this adventure called life.

If this brings tears, let them flow! Don't quickly wipe them away (ever). Tears are an incredibly healthy release valve, let them run in all their vulnerable beauty.

CONSCIOUS RELATIONSHIPS

Removing someone toxic from your life is one of the most empowering decisions we can make. It might be a friend, it might be a boss (the universe telling you to look for a new job), or it might be a lover. Whoever they are, if you surrendered, then took Inspired Action but their behavior did not change . . . They. Have. To. Go.

All relationships have a balance of power that was established early on (usually in the first six weeks). In the past seven weeks, you have made a massive internal shift, which these people haven't. Not surprisingly, the other person is going to wonder *what's going on?* If you haven't done this journal with friends or your partner, they are probably telling you you've changed. They may not mean it in a positive way, but take it as a compliment and thank them. (That'll mess with them.)

One of the greatest areas of sabotage in this aspect of our lives comes from our oldest relationships. Just because someone has been in your life since childhood doesn't mean they're exempt from all this positive change you've been making. If a person doesn't make you feel good, no matter how long you've known each other, self-respect dictates how you shift your relationship with them, either through speaking up, limiting, or cutting off contact. Cutting off contact doesn't have to be permanent. A three-month break is often all that is needed to energetically reset an unhealthy dynamic. Note: It has to be a total disconnect for three months. No contact at all. When I did this many years ago (I really do practice what I teach) I told my parents ahead of time what I was doing and why. Even though our relationship needed a reboot, worrying mum and dad by suddenly dropping off the radar wasn't honoring or respectful.

In the short term, quitting your job or totally dropping someone from your life may not be practical, so ask what you have a say in immediately. The answer usually lies in how much time and what sort of access you give this person. Think of the self-empowering end game with this relationship and in the weeks/months ahead, put into place the steps you need to take to get there. If you're starting to question your marriage, use your notes to look at how you feel when you're with your partner. In a healthy relationship, there will always be times where the dynamic drops, what you're looking for here are the patterns. Are you in any way contorting or diminishing yourself to keep the peace? How does your partner respond when you are completely, authentically yourself? How do they make you feel when you speak your truth, or do the things that make your heart sing?

Want to give marriage the best possible chance? Get to know who you really are *before* making this commitment. Have a life! Live abroad, pursue your career, fulfill some of those Lifelong Wishes. If marriage is an escape from, say, a boring job or a controlling family, no matter how much you love someone this unhealthy energy will be active in the relationship. You do know marriage will not make you happy? That's not its job. It's your job! Let's also drop any notions of "failure" when relationships end. We are constantly evolving, and expecting another person to grow at exactly the same rate isn't realistic. If you and your partner are no longer a vibrational match (that's what a relationship actually is) then the most authentically loving thing you can do is honor your expansion. Separately.

Tough Love: The two biggest traps that keep people in unhealthy relationships are children and money. If the mind comes up with children as an excuse, the best thing you can do for your kids is be an example of self-empowerment and self-respect. If the mind comes up with money as an excuse, what price are you willing to pay for your self-empowerment and self-respect?

A bit more Tough Love: If you are in the position of supporting extended family financially, it's time to change this unhealthy dynamic. With all the internal work you've now done, you'll understand why setting an end date or dollar cap for financial support is far more empowering than an endless cycle of handouts. Giving someone money indefinitely never leads to self-empowerment. If this is a really old dynamic it's unlikely you'll be able to make a big shift overnight. Small steps over the next six months will be more effective in bringing this relationship into a more empowering place. And yes, self-respect and self-empowerment aren't always popular.

A final form of sabotage the mind will come up with is along the lines of "if I practice these self-empowering exercises, I'll end up alone." Think of your relationships with others like a magnet. If the end of your magnet is full of disrespectful people, there won't be any room for healthy people. First you're going to have to make space for new relationships by removing people that no longer align with who you really are. Be okay with having an adjustment period, a time where you've gotten rid of the old but the new hasn't arrived yet. In many cases, you're shifting very old and unhealthy dynamics so it might take a while for truly healthy friendships to show up. There might even be some people who look healthy at the start and then turn out to be toxic. It's all a great learning experience. Just know you are much better served spending this time by yourself, and working on yourself, than allowing old dynamics to hold you back.

Inspired Action for an Empowered Endgame in my Unhealthy Relationships:

_____
_____
_____
_____
_____
_____
_____
_____
_____
_____
_____
_____
_____

CONSCIOUS CREATION

If career or finances is your greatest challenge, we're now going to do an exercise to uncover unconscious, unhealthy belief systems and then turn them around. Being realistic but reaching for the best possible outcome, write down a career or financial goal you'd like to achieve in the next six months. It can be an internal "I enjoy going to work every day," or an external "I am debt-free."* Using a notepad or sheets of paper, write down your desired outcome as a statement, and next to this write down the immediate emotional or mind response that comes up. As you begin, the response will usually be negative or maybe even nothing at all. It doesn't matter what you get, just write it down. Keep writing your statement/response until you feel excited or the inner voice says *yeah!* If your subconscious beliefs around this goal are really out of alignment with what you're asking for, it may take over an hour to get a positive response. Don't give up! In order for this exercise to work, you have to keep going until you get a positive response to the statement. Even if it starts out hugely negative, you will eventually turn it around. Promise!

P.S.: You can do this exercise for any area of your life.

* If you have credit card debt, every month as you pay the bill, send gratitude to the card for all things it has enabled you to enjoy.

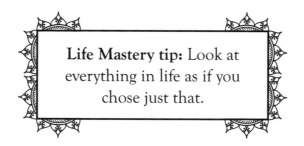

Life Mastery tip: Look at everything in life as if you chose just that.

We are energetic beings with six senses, not five. Call it instinct, intuition, or gut feeling, it is an essential part of who we are. If you're not embracing this aspect of yourself, you're like a six-cylinder car only operating on five cylinders.

Week 8 (Monday)

On a scale of 1–10, how do you feel about where your life is at right now? _____

Taking 5-10 minutes where you won't be interrupted, place a hand over your diaphragm and close your eyes. Take three deep breaths, breathing into the space behind your hand. I feel (don't forget, only write down the unpleasant emotions) . . .

_____
_____
_____
_____

Out loud, process any uncomfortable emotions:

    I allow myself to feel . . .
    I give myself permission to feel . . .
    I accept that I feel . . .
    The gifts and wisdom of feeling this way are . . .
    I make peace with feeling . . .
    I forgive/apologize to myself for feeling . . .
    I surrender to feeling . . .

Once you have processed the uncomfortable emotions, keeping your eyes closed, bring your right hand up above your head. Holding it an inch or two above your body, gently sweep down the front of your torso towards the legs. Then do the same with the left hand. As you continue sweeping over your body, you should feel a subtle, pleasant aliveness. This is your energetic body, life force energy, the essence of who you really are.

Week 8 affirmation: "I am life force energy in physical form and I choose how I create my external reality." When I say this out loud three times, I feel . . .

_____
_____
_____
_____

Week 8 (Tuesday)

Time required: whatever feels right for you

Place a hand over your diaphragm and close your eyes. Take three deep breaths, breathing into the space behind your hand. I feel (don't forget, only write down the unpleasant emotions) . . .

_____

_____

_____

_____

Out loud, process the uncomfortable emotions:

 I allow myself to feel . . .
 I give myself permission to feel . . .
 I accept that I feel . . .
 The gifts and wisdom of feeling this way are . . .
 I make peace with feeling . . .
 I forgive/apologize to myself for feeling . . .
 I surrender to feeling . . .

Like yesterday, keeping your eyes closed, place your right hand just above your head and gently stroke downwards. Then do the same with the left hand. Pay attention to the blissful, subtle "vibey" feeling you get.

I send gratitude to myself for overcoming this challenge . . . _____

_____

Week 8 affirmation: "I am life force energy in physical form and I choose how I create my external reality." When I say this out loud three times, I feel . . .

_____

_____

_____

Notes & Ideas:

_____

_____

Week 8 (Wednesday)

Time required: whatever feels right for you

Place a hand over your diaphragm and close your eyes. Take three deep breaths, breathing into the space behind your hand. I feel . . .

_____

_____

_____

_____

Out loud, process the uncomfortable emotions:

    I allow myself to feel . . .
    I give myself permission to feel . . .
    I accept that I feel . . .
    The gifts and wisdom of feeling this way are . . .
    I make peace with feeling . . .
    I forgive/apologize to myself for feeling . . .
    I surrender to feeling . . .

With your eyes closed, place your right hand above your head and gently stroke downwards. Then the left hand. The best description I have for the feeling is "warm fuzzies."

I feel so blessed for this part of my life . . . _____

_____

_____

_____

_____

Week 8 affirmation: "I am life force energy in physical form and I choose how I create my external reality." When I say this out loud three times, I feel . . .

_____

_____

_____

_____

Week 8 (Thursday)

Time required: whatever feels right for you

Place a hand over your diaphragm and close your eyes. Take three deep breaths, breathing into the space behind your hand. I feel . . .

_____

_____

_____

_____

Out loud, process the uncomfortable emotions:

I allow myself to feel . . .
I give myself permission to feel . . .
I accept that I feel . . .
The gifts and wisdom of feeling this way are . . .
I make peace with feeling . . .
I forgive/apologize to myself for feeling . . .
I surrender to feeling . . .

Stroke your energetic body, paying attention to how it feels.

I love this amazing experience called life because . . . _____

_____

Week 8 affirmation: "I am life force energy in physical form and I choose how I create my external reality." When I say this out loud three times, I feel . . .

_____

_____

_____

_____

Notes & Ideas:

_____

_____

_____

_____

Week 8 (Friday)

Time required: whatever feels right for you

Place a hand over your diaphragm and close your eyes. Take three deep breaths, breathing into the space behind your hand. I feel . . .

_____

_____

_____

_____

Out loud, process the uncomfortable emotions:

    I allow myself to feel . . .
    I give myself permission to feel . . .
    I accept that I feel . . .
    The gifts and wisdom of feeling this way are . . .
    I make peace with feeling . . .
    I forgive/apologize to myself for feeling . . .
    I surrender to feeling . . .

Take a few moments to gently stroke the energetic body, basking in the good vibes.

Today I am full of wonder and awe by . . . _____

_____

_____

Week 8 affirmation: "I am life force energy in physical form and I choose how I create my external reality." When I say this out loud three times, I feel . . .

_____

_____

_____

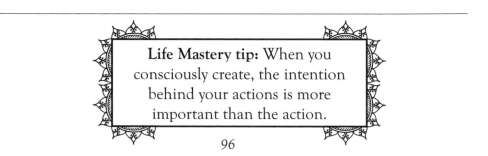

Life Mastery tip: When you consciously create, the intention behind your actions is more important than the action.

WEEKEND WORDS OF WISDOM

The energy that created universes flows through every cell in our bodies. If you want to live an empowered life, one of true freedom, you have to start honoring this energetic aspect of your being. Sanskrit texts talk of the center of our being as the sun in our galaxy. Many misinterpret this by thinking the sun center is your heart when in fact, and not surprisingly, it is your solar plexus. The energy-center of your being, where you can feel your connection to life force energy most strongly, is the area between the belly button and sternum. Home of your intuition and gut feel, the third chakra in Hinduism . . . also that place you've been placing your hand every weekday doing the Intuitive Healing process.

As you would have noticed with the morning "stroking" exercise, the feeling of our energetic body is very subtle. Mind chatter and external distractions make it difficult to tune in to. Old emotional wounds, insecurities, and unhealthy belief systems also mar this connection, which is why you've spent the past eight weeks healing and transforming the emotional body.

The word "psychic" comes from the Greek word *psukhé* which means breath, or life. The ancient Greeks (smart buggers!) considered the psyche to be the spiritual aspect of a human being. The word "clairvoyant" comes from French and means clear vision. Clair = clear. Part of my gift is clairsentience, from the latin word *sentire*, which means to feel. I can feel different energy, which I prefer to seeing it, as clairvoyance sometimes freaks me out. One of my cousins has clairolfactance, the ability to smell energy. I can also hear energy, clairaudience, and frequently have claircognizance, what I call a "knowing." The bottom line here is an attunement or sensitivity to see, hear, smell, feel, beyond the physical. A better word than psychic would be "sensitive." A sensitivity to the vibrating energy which everything is made of.

For those of you who have thought of yourselves as overly sensitive, there is no such thing. You are most likely one of the clairs above, and simply not empowered in your energetic body. Everyone, to varying degrees, has some form of psychic sensitivity, they've just never been taught how to use it. Until now . . .

EMBRACING YOUR ENERGETIC SELF

Our energetic body is a stream of consciousness or life force energy that constantly flows through us. To fully connect with this aspect of our being you first need to disengage from the constant chatter of the mind. The best time to practice this is when you are about to fall asleep or have just woken up (provided it's not an alarm jolting you out of sleep). Lie still, with your eyes closed, bringing your focus to the space from your solar plexus up the sternum, radiating out to the upper arms. From deep inside to about an inch above the skin. You're reaching into "feeling" your energy, not your physical or emotional body, but the essence of who you are. As the "stroking" exercise showed, it's a gentle, vibey aliveness.

When you first tune in to the energetic body it may only be for a fleeting moment. Hold your awareness on this blissful space for as long as you can. Like exercising a muscle, you have to practice tuning into this energy to strengthen the connection. Your homework is to do this exercise daily, either just before falling asleep or when you first wake up (whichever works best for you.)

Heads up: The energetic body only ever feels gently relaxing and blissful. If you feel any discomfort, that's your emotional body.

How are you doing with actioning one of your Lifelong Wishes? If your partner or friends keep telling you how impossible one of your wishes is, stop talking to them about it. Don't take advice from someone who hasn't experienced or at least attempted the wish. It's important to surround yourself with supportive people, and one of the easiest ways to align with your wishes is to connect with people who have done it.

YOUR DIVINE PHYSICAL SELF

One of the best ways to honor your divine physical self is to swim naked in nature. The degree of difficulty (and legality) this entails depends on where you are in the world. Living in Berlin, I could strip to my heart's content, and still do. If swimming naked in a forest lake isn't possible, what about a local Korean or Roman bathhouse? Or jumping in your own pool under a full moon? You get to skip the mirror exercise this week (thank me later!), instead your homework is to find somewhere, legal and noncreepy, you can take your body and be naked. Bonus points for doing this with other naked people. This is one of those exercises you won't know how liberating and good it feels until you try it.

Story Time: when I first visited the lakes of Berlin, I was really shocked to see everyone just strip off and jump in. Even though I grew up on the topless beaches of Australia, the closest to fully naked strangers I'd seen were models. No wonder the average person has so much body shame! By the lakes of Germany I saw every type of body: young, old, fat, skinny, stretch marked, pregnant, flabby, toned, you name it, the human form in all its variations. And in less than an hour, my naked-assed self didn't see anything odd about it.

CONSCIOUS RELATIONSHIPS

If you have disrespectful people in your life, the energetic law of balance says you most likely have some people you're a bit of an asshole to as well. On the following page, write down the people you don't always treat so well. Next to their names, put exactly how you treat them. It might be uncomfortable, but be honest about your own bad behavior. How do you feel when you're treating them badly? Frustrated? Annoyed? Tired? Add this to your list. (If you're not sure, pay attention when you spend time together.) Then process these feelings through to surrender.

Why do you have these people in your circle? If there's guilt, you know that's not empowering for either of you, go below the guilt (e.g., "I feel sorry for them") and process those emotions. Sympathy has an element of judgement in it and is never empowering. Yes, I just said sympathy is not empowering. Empathy, however, derives from compassion, and is empowering. There's a subtle but big difference* between these two, which you should now be able to feel. By surrendering to this aspect of your behavior, you'll come up with some Inspired Action you can take to shift this unhealthy dynamic. Just as you removed disrespectful people from your life, if you can't shift your dynamic to be nicer and kinder to everyone in your circle, the most honoring thing you can do for both of you, is to distance yourself.

* Every word in every language has its own unique energetic vibration, which is a combination of the meaning of the word as well as how you feel as you are speaking it. When the meaning and feeling are in alignment, the words we speak have the power to influence our reality. As you speak, you are pouring energy out into your surroundings. The question is, are you putting health out into your surroundings or are you polluting them? I will not let people complain when talking with me because it's verbal pollution. Like its near cousin, blaming, complaining is the act of a coward, someone who refuses to take responsibility.

Heads up: Complaining about the weather is one of the most unevolved things we can do. The weather is neither good nor bad, it's just mother nature in all her glory and our interpretation of it. Cold winter days should be celebrated, because the following spring will have a marked drop in illness, as freezing temperatures kill off bacteria and viruses. Rain brings life. Next time it rains, put away your umbrella, lift your head and celebrate this unique manifestation (only planet in the universe!) of life-bringing energy.

The People I Can do Better With:

_____
_____
_____
_____
_____
_____
_____
_____
_____
_____
_____
_____
_____
_____
_____

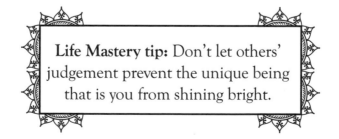

Life Mastery tip: Don't let others' judgement prevent the unique being that is you from shining bright.

CONSCIOUS CREATION

"Dear god, I need a million dollars" is destined for failure because the energy around this sort of prayer is usually one of neediness and lack. By expecting some guy in the sky to drop cash on you and solve your problems, you also remain disempowered. Now imagine instead, you took something that represented abundance (say, a green candle) and put a little oil on it that has the vibration of attraction (like lodestone oil). Then you lit that candle every night for a week, burning it down a little at a time, while focusing on all the ways you already have prosperity in your life and how amazing this feels. You then took some sage (representing cleansing) and lit it until it smoked, waving the smoke all around your body, while saying "I release all blocks and barriers, opening myself up and allowing life force energy to fully flow through me." Before blowing out the candle, you said (and meant it) words to the effect of "show me what I need to do to align with abundance consciousness, reveal my blind spots, make the unconscious conscious, so I might heal and grow."

In the days and weeks ahead, you were then to pay close attention to how you felt about money, wealth, or anything related to prosperity. Every challenging emotion you processed, and every challenging situation, you asked, "what can I learn from this?" Every time you saw an example of abundance consciousness you wrote it down and then basked in those feelings. You never focused on the outcome, only on the process. What you'd come to realize as you grew and healed is that abundance isn't about money at all (although an abundance consciousness easily attracts money), it's about something far more profound, but you'll have to do this exercise to discover it for yourself. Hint: it has to do with an open heart.

Tough love: Consciously asking the universe, god, (whatever you wish to call it) for help or guidance also means being at peace when things don't turn out as your mind wishes.

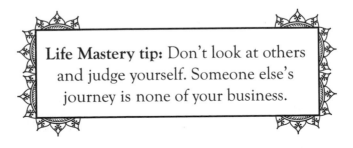

Life Mastery tip: Don't look at others and judge yourself. Someone else's journey is none of your business.

Think of yourself as the captain of a ship. You can't control the ocean or the weather, but you get to choose where you sail. Life Mastery is to consciously and intentionally navigate the seas of life.

Week 9 (Monday)

On a scale of 1–10, how do you feel about where your life is at right now? _____

Taking 5–10 minutes where you won't be interrupted, place a hand over your diaphragm and close your eyes. Take three deep breaths, breathing into the space behind your hand. I feel (say everything but only write down the uncomfortable emotions) . . .

_____

_____

_____

_____

Out loud, process the uncomfortable emotions:

    I allow myself to feel . . .
    I give myself permission to feel . . .
    I accept that I feel . . .
    The gifts and wisdom of feeling this way are . . .
    I make peace with feeling . . .
    I forgive/apologize to myself for feeling . . .
    I surrender to feeling . . .

Once you process the challenging emotions, tune into that vibey, warm fuzzy space you're practicing finding every morning or night. Enjoy this connection for as long as you can hold it. If stroking the energy helps, and you can do it without feeling self-conscious, do that as well.

Week 9 affirmation: "My life is rich and abundant in . . ." (you're going to name three different things every day)

_____

_____

_____

Notes & Ideas:

_____

_____

Week 9 (Tuesday)

Time required: whatever feels right for you.

Place a hand over your diaphragm and close your eyes. Take three deep breaths, breathing into the space behind your hand. I feel (say everything but only write down the uncomfortable emotions) . . .

_____
_____
_____
_____

Out loud, process any uncomfortable emotions:

I allow myself to feel . . .
I give myself permission to feel . . .
I accept that I feel . . .
The gifts and wisdom of feeling this way are . . .
I make peace with feeling . . .
I forgive/apologize to myself for feeling . . .
I surrender to feeling . . .

Tune into your energetic body. Stroke it if that helps, enjoy this connection for as long as you can.

Week 9 affirmation: "My life is rich and abundant in . . ." (three different things every day)

_____
_____
_____
_____

Notes & Ideas:

_____
_____
_____

Week 9 (Wednesday)

Time required: whatever feels right for you.

Place a hand over your diaphragm and close your eyes. Take three deep breaths, breathing into the space behind your hand. I feel (say everything but only write down the uncomfortable emotions) . . .

_____

_____

_____

_____

Out loud, process any uncomfortable emotions:

> I allow myself to feel . . .
> I give myself permission to feel . . .
> I accept that I feel . . .
> The gifts and wisdom of feeling this way are . . .
> I make peace with feeling . . .
> I forgive/apologize to myself for feeling . . .
> I surrender to feeling . . .

Once you've processed any uncomfortable emotions find that vibey feeling that is your energetic body. Stroking the energy if that works for you.

Week 9 affirmation: "My life is rich and abundant in . . ." (three different things every day)

_____

_____

_____

_____

Notes & Ideas:

_____

_____

_____

Week 9 (Thursday)

Time required: whatever feels right for you.

Place a hand over your diaphragm and close your eyes. Take three deep breaths, breathing into the space behind your hand. I feel (say everything but only write down the uncomfortable emotions) . . .

_____

_____

_____

_____

Out loud, process any uncomfortable emotions:

> I allow myself to feel . . .
> I give myself permission to feel . . .
> I accept that I feel . . .
> The gifts and wisdom of feeling this way are . . .
> I make peace with feeling . . .
> I forgive/apologize to myself for feeling . . .
> I surrender to feeling . . .

Tune in to the warm fuzzy feeling that is your energetic body, holding this blissful connection for as long as you can.

Week 9 affirmation: "My life is rich and abundant in . . ." (three different things every day)

_____

_____

_____

_____

Notes & Ideas:

_____

_____

_____

Week 9 (Friday)

Time required: whatever feels right for you.

Place a hand over your diaphragm and close your eyes. Take three deep breaths, breathing into the space behind your hand. I feel (say everything but only write down the uncomfortable emotions) . . .

_____

_____

_____

_____

Out loud, process any uncomfortable emotions:

> I allow myself to feel . . .
> I give myself permission to feel . . .
> I accept that I feel . . .
> The gifts and wisdom of feeling this way are . . .
> I make peace with feeling . . .
> I forgive/apologize to myself for feeling . . .
> I surrender to feeling . . .

Find that high vibrational essence of your energetic self and bask in it.

Week 9 affirmation: "My life is rich and abundant in . . ." (three new things)

_____

_____

_____

_____

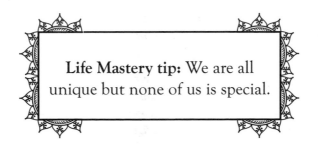

Life Mastery tip: We are all unique but none of us is special.

WEEKEND WORDS OF WISDOM

Time to get the external world working for you by supporting your bliss! An outdated (and dare I say, religious) idea is that one can't reach spiritual enlovement without denouncing worldly pleasures. When doing what makes you happy is actually one of the surest ways to get into alignment with life force energy. This isn't putting on rose-colored glasses—if you just follow your bliss without doing any inner work, old wounds and unhealthy belief systems will still be active vibrationally.

So, do your inner work then follow your bliss!

Let's assume you're doing your inner work (if you're this far through the journal, you are) then it's time to lighten up and start doing more of what makes you feel good. You don't need a great deal of money or time (the two great saboteurs) to do this. Sing along to the radio, dance to your favorite song, sit out in the sunshine. Anything that makes you smile and laugh, strengthens your alignment with life force energy and who you authentically are. And here's the good news: as you do things that bring you more and more into alignment, more things, experiences and opportunities, that strengthen this connection even further will come your way!

Tough Love: Drop any ideas you might have around the tortured artist. You should now know, if you create from anxiety or suffering, then you just are spreading more anxiety and suffering.

Story Time: When I first began doing this work, I didn't believe in reincarnation. Because the universe has a sense of humor, I have since seen so much evidence that we have been here before and we get to come back. Years ago, I fainted in a ceramic shop. While blacked out, they began scraping the pottery up and in my mind's eye I vividly saw myself working on the pyramids. The sun was beating down on my blackened skin and I was starved and exhausted. Surrounded by thousands of other slaves, I knew I'd died there.

When a newborn baby looks like an old man, you're actually seeing the energetic imprint of their last physical form. Furthermore, we do make soul agreements but they are not what most people think. We don't have soul mates*, as in one person and only one person for you. There is the perfect person for you right now, subject to change. A soul agreement is more likely to be with your abuser than your lover. You might want to read that sentence again. The person who brought you unimaginable pain is the catalyst for you to begin this journey to reconnect with your authentic self—that's a soul agreement.

*don't get me started on the bullshit of twin flames!

SUI GENERIS

The unique being that is you has never existed before and will never exist again. That's how extraordinary you are! Want to know what you came into this physical time-space reality to do? Start by bringing the genuine expression of yourself out into the planet. Where in your life are you censoring yourself? In what ways are you hiding your eccentric, quirky self in order to fit in? And how has that worked out for you so far? In order to connect with who you authentically are, you have to start honoring your uniqueness. Trying to fit in or hide parts of our true nature is also exhausting. Being authentic might feel scary at first, but eventually it will feel liberating and energizing.

All these exercises in this journal have been guiding you, step-by-step, to reconnect with your authentic self. You know another name for this self-empowering condition? Unconditional love, a concept we've all heard of but very few truly practice. Embracing and honoring the aspects of you that are different, is a form of self-love. You now know all creation begins within, which means you can't completely accept others' differences if you are hiding, ashamed, or rejecting your own. Want to be a better partner, parent, or leader? Start by loving all of yourself: the good, the bad . . . and the weird.

One of the greatest forms of dishonoring our unique being is hiding our psychic senses. If you have a particular intuitive gift you've kept hidden, it's time to come out of the (broom) closet. This natural aspect of our being comes in many variations and combinations, all as unique as we are. I know a man in Crete who can sense where there is underground water, and a lady in Texas who intuits the weather better than The Weather Channel. Whatever energetic gift you have, it's life force energy directly expressing itself through you. Using your gift is not only self-empowering, it'll open the flood gates, allowing more life force to flow into other areas of your life. You'll also be aligning with your life's true purpose . . . so no biggie!

If you're having an *ah-ha* moment as you read this and know just what sort of unique gift you have, write it down. Get specific on what happens and when it is triggered. You may be about to name things you've never told anyone, so be brave. Your mind might tell you, you're making it up or it's a useless gift. Ignore it. If the ego gets involved and tells you you're special or better than others, ignore that as well! Life force energy only ever unites, it never separates. One of the best parts of teaching workshops is seeing students open up to their gifts. Your homework in the week ahead is to actively put yourself around people or situations that act as triggers to your gift and see what happens.

Heads up: It's smart to be skeptical. If I hadn't experienced the magic and power of the energetic body, my science-trained mind wouldn't believe any of it. But when you witness something inexplicable, it's the opposite of smart to continue to close yourself off from this aspect of life. The mind is very quick to dismiss, or worse still, reject our energetic body by judging it as bad. We come from pure positive life force energy and we return to pure positive life force energy. The energetic body is not only natural, it's who we originally are. One of the best ways to counter your inner skeptic is to keep a written record of every odd little thing that happens. It's often only when we look back and see a long list of small things, that we begin to see all our energetic gift has to offer.

Bonus Homework: If you're not sure you have an intuitive gift or just want to ramp up your connection to the energetic body, angel decks or tarot cards are hands down your best tool to start with.

To get the most bang for your buck with the cards:
1. Pick a deck that appeals you.
2. "Charge" the deck by going through the information booklet and holding each card while reading out loud and feeling the meaning.
3. Above all, have fun!

How you choose to spend your two "self" hours each week is the perfect time to give expression to your singular self. If learning the trapeze makes you giddy with excitement, go for it! Always had a desire to speak Swahili, get it on! Whatever calls to you, whatever makes your heart sing and your body come alive, do it!

Unique aspects of my divine being I have been hiding or ashamed of:

_____

_____

_____

_____

Empowering ways I can begin to express this part of myself:

_____

_____

_____

_____

Some weird and wonderful things have happened since I began honoring my energetic self . . .

_____

_____

_____

_____

YOUR DIVINE PHYSICAL SELF

Congratulations on how far you've come with your relationship with the physical aspect of your divine being! How well we accept compliments is a great indicator of our internal self-respect. How did you feel as you read the congratulatory message?

_____

_____

_____

Rituals are a way for us to honor and respect the sacred aspect of life. Raising your glass and saying "cheers" or "salut" is a ritual. Singing "Happy Birthday" is another ritual. In the past nine weeks, you've done an internal reset on your relationship with yourself. A great way to honor this healthy newfound relationship is, you guessed it, with a ritual.

Do this around the full moon. Read back over your notes regarding your relationship with yourself, both the internal and external. On a loose piece of paper, write out all the ways that you were once harsh, judgmental, or critical of yourself. Light a candle, strip down, and look at your beautiful body in the mirror (you didn't think we'd skip the mirror two weeks in a row, did you?) Hold the list and look at your body, saying words to the effect of "I'm sorry I once felt this way about you. I now know you are my divine light in physical form. I release all destructive, critical thoughts and beliefs, so this energy may recycle itself back to white light and pure love." Burn that bit of paper from the candle. Take a bath, exfoliate your skin (off with the old!) and wash your hair. As you wash and later dry yourself off, be very conscious of how you touch your body. You want to be as gentle and loving as you would a child's body. Then put on something that represents this new relationship with yourself. It could be a favorite item of clothing, a beloved piece of jewelry, or a new way of styling your hair. (If this is your second read of the journal, redo these rituals honoring the different time of year and your deeper connection with yourself.)

Story Time: I did yoga, bored senseless, for decades, and it wasn't until I started Brazilian jiujitsu that I realized what I was missing. I sweat like crazy, my hair is a mess, but my body positively hums on the jiujitsu mat! Doing exercise that makes your body come alive honors your unique being, so don't be afraid to try new things around your health and fitness.

CONSCIOUS CREATION

We all have energetic blueprints that were established very early on (usually the first seven years) in our lives. At their most basic, blueprints will either be one of receiving or resisting. If you grew up in an environment where you felt safe and nurtured, where the majority of the energy that surrounded you was supportive and loving, then you will have "receiving" blueprints. On the other hand, if you grew up in an unsafe environment, if you were bullied or abandoned, or the energy that surrounded you wasn't positive, then you will have "resisting" blueprints.

We can have different blueprints for different areas of our lives. If manifesting in the physical world, like a great job or plenty of money, always feels like an uphill battle, then chances are you have a resisting blueprint for career and finances. The gift of this blueprint is healthy boundaries. Resistance energy also makes for more discernment, someone who prefers quality over quantity, as well as a deeper appreciation for things you have manifested.

If you're in receiving mode for career and finances, then manifesting in the physical world will come quite easily. The downside is you can have too much of a good thing. People with a receiving blueprint struggle to say no, whether to people and events, or shopping and pleasure. Receivers are often surrounded by too much stuff and have people in their lives who overstep their boundaries.

If you have a resistance blueprint around career, you are going to have to stay very conscious of how you feel when you think of putting yourself up for a promotion or going to a job interview. If you are in resistance around finances, you have to stay conscious of how you feel as you look at your bank balance, spend money, or look at things you presently can't afford. What you feel isn't going to be pleasant. The resistance blueprint is a form of protection, your energetic body protecting you from pain as a child. When you feel the discomfort, stay present in it and then speak to that part of yourself. Thank it for keeping you safe, then let it know you no longer need protecting, that this energy is now causing more harm than good and you release it back to life force energy.

If you are in receiving mode, then you are going to have to practice saying no to people, more shoes, or needing to have the latest gadget when the old one is working perfectly. Whatever it is that you have far too much of in your life, if you want healthy balance, the time has come to say no. Just like the resisters, it will feel unpleasant when you first begin to put up boundaries, stay present in the feelings, thanking that part of yourself for all the abundance it has bought you, then explain how this is now causing more harm than good, and why saying no is necessary and empowering. In your mind's eye, imagine putting up healthy boundaries in this part of your life.

Whether you're a resister or a receiver, this exercise has to be done when the energy is active. I'm not going to BS you, this can be hard to do! You have to wait for the energy to be activated, which doesn't feel good, then stay in the discomfort and communicate with it.

If you lie awake at night stressing out, instead of getting frustrated, see it as a great opportunity to work on a blueprint. Sink down into the stress and then say, "it is my intention to heal and release this blueprint, replacing it with trust" (stress is a form of fear, the opposite of fear is trust). Then, speak to your anxiety, saying you understand why it's there and how it's trying to help. Genuinely thank it and tell that part of yourself you love it but now it's time to release it back to life force energy. In your mind's eye, see the stress releasing and then feel the new blueprint, in this case self-trust, establishing itself as you say out loud, "I trust myself." You can play around with different wording as you work through this exercise.

When we are born, we *need* attention. It's the energy of attention that actually draws part of our nonphysical energetic self into the physical body. Touch also provides this life-sustaining pull. By giving the young attention and affection, you ground their energetic selves in their physical bodies. If you didn't get enough attention as a kid or you got unhealthy attention (abuse), there will be an underlying void deep within, which will show up as neediness or in its most destructive form, addiction. To heal this void you're going to have to sit in the yearning or craving when it's active and talk to that aspect of yourself, then consciously "feed" yourself the loving energy you missed out on. For those of you with this most challenging of energetic blueprints, forgive yourself for any unhealthy ways you may have tried to fill this void in the past.

Bonus Homework: Look up at the night sky and pay attention to how you feel. You are looking out into an ever-expanding universe and you should feel the pull of your consciousness recognizing itself in that expansion.

Don't fear death, because it's really a returning or a homecoming. Scientists say energy is neither created nor destroyed, it just changes form. Well, we are all energy, and death is simply a return to form.

Week 10 (Monday)

On a scale of 1-10, how do you feel about where your life is at right now? _____

Taking 5-10 minutes where you won't be interrupted, place a hand over your diaphragm and close your eyes. Take three deep breaths, breathing into the space behind your hand. I feel (name everything, write down the uncomfortable emotions) . . .

_____

_____

_____

_____

Out loud, process the uncomfortable emotions:

> I allow myself to feel . . .
> I give myself permission to feel . . .
> I accept that I feel . . .
> The gifts and wisdom of feeling this way are . . .
> I make peace with feeling . . .
> I forgive/apologize to myself for feeling . . .
> I surrender to feeling . . .

Find that warm fuzzy feeling and enjoy the alignment with your energetic body. If there is still any unease or discomfort, *observe* it while still holding your alignment, recognizing the unease is not who you really are.

Today I practiced being authentic by . . . _____

Want to hear some excellent news? Being authentic will attract more authentic people around you!

Week 10 affirmation: There is no right way or wrong way to connect with and communicate to life force energy. Write this in your own words (I left space Tuesday–Friday) "To the greater part of me that is life force energy, I love, love, love, this adventure we are on. As I go throughout my day, show me a sign and bring it in such a way I will not doubt that you are with me, loving me, guiding me, cheering me on." When I say this out loud three times, I feel . . .

_____

_____

_____

Week 10 (Tuesday)

Time required: up to you

Place a hand over your diaphragm and close your eyes. Take three deep breaths, breathing into the space behind your hand. I feel (name everything, write down the uncomfortable emotions) . . .

_____

_____

_____

_____

Out loud, process any uncomfortable emotions:

> I allow myself to feel . . .
> I give myself permission to feel . . .
> I accept that I feel . . .
> The gifts and wisdom of feeling this way are . . .
> I make peace with feeling . . .
> I forgive/apologize to myself for feeling . . .
> I surrender to feeling . . .

Bask in the bliss of your energetic body. Observe any unpleasant feelings if they are still there, like ripples on the surface of the ocean as you dive deeper and deeper.

Do you have an odd sense of humor? Like to dress in out-there clothes? In what ways, both big and small, aren't you being authentic and allowing your light to shine bright?

Today, I will practice authenticity by . . . _____

_____

_____

_____

_____

Write down your affirmation, say it out loud three times, then write down how it makes you feel:

_____

_____

_____

Week 10 (Wednesday)

Time required: up to you

Place a hand over your diaphragm and close your eyes. Take three deep breaths, breathing into the space behind your hand. I feel (name everything, write down the uncomfortable emotions) . . .

_____

_____

_____

_____

Out loud, process any uncomfortable emotions:

    I allow myself to feel . . .
    I give myself permission to feel . . .
    I accept that I feel . . .
    The gifts and wisdom of feeling this way are . . .
    I make peace with feeling . . .
    I forgive/apologize to myself for feeling . . .
    I surrender to feeling . . .

Tune into the pure positive life force energy that is who you really are. Hold that feeling for as long as you can while observing any residual feelings that aren't in alignment with your authentic energetic self.

Today I will be my authentic, quirky self by . . . _____

_____

_____

_____

_____

Write down your affirmation, say it out loud three times, then write down how it makes you feel:

_____

_____

_____

_____

Week 10 (Thursday)

Time required: up to you

Place a hand over your diaphragm and close your eyes. Take three deep breaths, breathing into the space behind your hand. I feel (name everything, write down the uncomfortable emotions) . . .

_____

_____

_____

_____

Out loud, process any uncomfortable emotions:

> I allow myself to feel . . .
> I give myself permission to feel . . .
> I accept that I feel . . .
> The gifts and wisdom of feeling this way are . . .
> I make peace with feeling . . .
> I forgive/apologize to myself for feeling . . .
> I surrender to feeling . . .

Bask in the vibey aliveness of your energetic body. Simply observe anything that is not in alignment with who you really are.

Having an opinion is an aspect of authenticity. Where in your life do you keep your point of view to yourself? By voicing your opinions, even if others don't vibe them, you are giving expression to the unique being that is you . . . which is doing your soul's work.

Today I will practice authenticity by . . . _____

_____

_____

_____

Write down your affirmation, say it out loud three times, then write down how it makes you feel:

_____

_____

_____

Week 10 (Friday)

Time required: up to you

Place a hand over your diaphragm and close your eyes. Take three deep breaths, breathing into the space behind your hand. I feel (name everything, write down the uncomfortable emotions) . . .

_____

_____

_____

_____

Out loud, process any uncomfortable emotions:

I allow myself to feel . . .
I give myself permission to feel . . .
I accept that I feel . . .
The gifts and wisdom of feeling this way are . . .
I make peace with feeling . . .
I forgive/apologize to myself for feeling . . .
I surrender to feeling . . .

Revel in the good vibes of your energetic body. Separate yourself from any lingering unease by observing it.

My authentic being will shine bright today when I . . . _____

_____

Write down your affirmation, say it out loud three times, then write down how it makes you feel:

_____

_____

_____

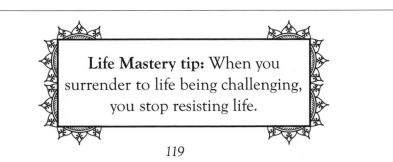

Life Mastery tip: When you surrender to life being challenging, you stop resisting life.

WEEKEND WORDS OF WISDOM

I wasn't trying to impress you with my poetic genius when I began the weekday meditations with, "I can't promise smooth sailing, but I can make you a better sailor." A trap many of us fall into, myself included, is thinking that once we reach some enlovened state, life will be all ease and flow and grace. Not true. Life was meant to be challenging!

Physicists tell us we live in an ever-expanding universe, what they're yet to work out is that our consciousness is part of the driving force behind that expansion. Part of the reason life force energy became physical was for the opportunities of growth and expansion that the physical plane offers. You with me on this? You came here to grow and evolve. And the catalyst for this expansion is the challenges we face. Once you embrace challenges as essential, you see them for what they really are: friend, not foe.

YOUR MOST IMPORTANT RELATIONSHIP

Once you surrender and reconnect with your blissful energetic body, old pain may still be present. The self-empowering trick here is realizing any old pain is but a tiny speck of dust on the vast luminous being that you are. When you observe the speck, while holding fast to the limitlessness that is really you, you stop feeding old pain the energy it needs to stay active. The pain will eventually dissolve and recycle into life force energy, but it can't do this when there is any resistance.

As you work through this journal on your second read through, your body might ache at night. Sometimes it will feel like your very bones are sore or the top layer of skin is being pinched. This is the accumulated energy of emotional wounds coming to the surface and releasing. It may hurt like hell but it's a really positive sign. Focus on the discomfort and in your mind's eye, see the pain flowing out of your body, recycling back to Source energy. Stroke the energetic body (like in morning meditation) and imagine pulling the hurt out and releasing it. This type of pain usually comes in waves, not dissimilar to labor.

CONSCIOUS WORKOUTS

Exercise is a great way to physically support the release of old emotional wounds. When you work out, pay attention to how you feel. If you have any anger, frustration, or uncomfortable emotions, start with low impact, flow exercise like swimming, spinning, or yin yoga, setting the intention of releasing this energy. Only once you're feeling good should you start any high impact or muscle building exercise. How you feel as you build muscle will be stored in your muscle memory, so pay attention.

Old, unhealed emotional wounds will often manifest physically (like how my numbed heartache became neck pain), not to punish you but to bring your attention to this hurt so you can heal it. Not every physical disease is emotionally based, but if you have some ailment that defies traditional medicine, gently rub your hand over that part of your body and tune in to how it feels. If you have old injuries or have had surgery, gently rub your hand there and feel if there's any old pain still present. If there is, talk to the wound, asking what it needs to heal. You may not get an answer right away but be on the lookout for anything that comes your way in the weeks ahead, be it a type of food, a new exercise or healing practice, or maybe running into someone from your past. Women who get painful monthly cramps without an underlying medical condition should start celebrating their fertility and connection to nature every month and see what happens.

What my old wounds asked for, for healing:

_____
_____
_____
_____

We're going to skip your new friend the mirror this week (I know you're disappointed), instead your homework is to get some bodywork (massage, acupuncture, kinesiology) that supports the release of old pain. Do your research and make sure the practitioner is conscious and healthy. If you're unsure, feel out the words they use on their website and look at how they treat their own body. Enjoy!

THE WEIRD AND WONDERFUL

If there is anything you own that reminds you of, or if you were wearing it at the time of a painful event, it either needs to be cleansed or gotten rid of. Jewelry in particular accumulates energy, especially jewelry with gemstones. If you have a piece you wear often or something you inherited or bought vintage, you should cleanse the energy of the item. If you don't, no matter how beautiful, you are carrying energetic baggage around with you.

Here are some ways to clear energy, do what feels right for the piece in question:

1. Place under a full moon overnight.
2. Soak in salt water from the ocean.
3. Place out in the sun's rays.

Metal blocks the flow of energy, so remove any jewelry when you go to bed at night.

Sleep isn't just for our physical bodies, it's also how the energetic body recharges. Your bedroom should be peaceful and vibrationally clear, if there's anything that doesn't feel right, take some Inspired Action to shift things around. This includes paying attention to the energy of people you share your bed with. We are bombarded with all sorts of energy waves throughout the day, so turn your mobile phone and Wi-Fi router off at night. And if you've been taking sleeping tablets long-term, you're stopping the energetic body from recharging properly—work the Intuitive Healing process around the real issue disrupting your sleep.

As you become more attuned to your energetic body, you will become more sensitive to the external world. Don't be put off by this. If you find yourself in a situation that feels overwhelming, pressing your thumb to your middle finger on each hand will close off your energetic field, protecting you. If the space where you live or work doesn't have a good vibe, smudging sage, flicking salt water with your fingers or different types of crystals are your friends. I also suggest taking a white light shower (visualize it) at the end of any energy work, setting the intention of washing away anything that doesn't serve the highest good.

RELATIONSHIPS WITH OTHER LANDS

In the last 200 years, there has been so much migration that many of us grew up in countries that are not our energetic land. Years ago, a Scottish guy asked me if I "missed my land?" At the time, I had no idea what he was talking about. Did I miss the beaches of Sydney? Sure, but not enough to stop me from living abroad. It's the experience I'm about to share with you that actually opened me up to what he was really asking.

A wee bit of background: my maternal great-grandparents are Scots. In 1996, I moved to Scotland and decided to walk the spectacular West Highland Way. One hundred and fifty-ish kilometers, starting in Glasgow and finishing at Ben Nevis, Britain's highest mountain. You first view the highlands by climbing a steep rocky ridge known as the Devil's Staircase. This is from my journal: "At the top of the

Devil's Staircase, the breathtaking Highlands opened up in front of me. As I stood there taking in the view (and catching my breath), the earth began to talk to me. This warm, loving embrace came up through my hiking boots, soared up my legs and filled my entire body. I got goosebumps as I heard the whispers of my ancestors saying 'welcome home, dear one, welcome home.' The energy was so strong I ended up on my knees, crying. Thankfully there were no other hikers about! When I finally pulled myself together, I headed down the path into a forest, and the wind through the fir trees continued the whispered welcome."

To this day, this is one of the most profound and intense experiences of my life (and I've seen some weird shit go down). If you grew up in the new world, visit your ancestral homeland. If you have an inexplicable desire to see a certain foreign country, chances are you have a past life connection that is calling you. (Bonus points if this is one of the Lifelong Wishes you're already actioning.) To experience a spiritual connection to the land is truly sacred. It has also given me a deeper appreciation and respect for indigenous cultures and the importance of honoring their connection to the land.

CONSCIOUS CREATION

Because we rarely make quantum shifts vibrationally, it's unlikely big opportunities will appear out of the blue (and like lottery winnings, you'd probably blow them just as quickly). Having an endgame in mind helps stay your course when things get challenging. And as you now know, things will always be challenging. You've done enough inner work to understand that an external endgame, like being rich or important, is pure ego, while an internal endgame along the lines of contributing to the greater good or bringing your unique gifts out into the world, is more aligned with who you really are. This isn't to say a bit of bling isn't fun, it's aligned with abundance consciousness after all, but see it for what it really is: candy floss, not the deeply fulfilling meal you're seeking.

The reason we want to manifest anything is because of how we think we will feel by having it. Read that sentence again. Everything we want, is because of how we think we will feel when we get it. Life Mastery is to have the internals (feelings) irrespective of external conditions. You might want to reread that as well.

If you switch your desires to the internal state you think they will give you, and then appreciate the areas in your life where you already get these feelings, you will quickly and easily begin to manifest the things you are asking for (assuming you released any blocks by doing the end of week 8 homework). Take your career or financial goals and redefine them internally.

How manifesting my career and/or financial desires will make me feel:

_____

_____

_____

_____

_____

_____

_____

_____

Circle two or three internals you most desire and turn it into an intention: e.g., "It is my intention to feel creative, free, and energized." This will be next week's affirmation.

Tough Love: Many people sabotage receiving what they've been asking for by judging how it shows up. Opportunities usually come in unexpected ways, from unexpected quarters. More of a side step that might be fun to try for a bit, than an obvious leap forward. Being in receiving mode means being open to what shows up and saying yes, even if you don't know exactly where it's going to take you. If reading these words makes you realize you've missed out on some of life's opportunities, don't sweat it! If something was meant to be, it will come back around.

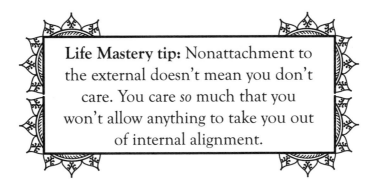

Life Mastery tip: Nonattachment to the external doesn't mean you don't care. You care *so* much that you won't allow anything to take you out of internal alignment.

A man stands in a building, lights candles, burns incense, says a chant, and it's called a holy prayer. A woman stands in a forest, lights candles, burns incense, says a chant, and it's called an evil spell. Go figure?

Week 11 (Monday)

On a scale of 1–10, how do you feel about where your life is at right now? _____

Taking 5–10 minutes where you won't be interrupted, place a hand over your diaphragm and close your eyes. Take three deep breaths, breathing into the space behind your hand.

I feel . . .

_____
_____
_____
_____

You should now be able to process any uncomfortable emotions, out loud, without having to read the steps.

I allow myself to feel . . .
I give myself permission to feel . . .
I accept that I feel . . .
The gifts and wisdom of feeling this way are . . .
I make peace with feeling . . .
I forgive/apologize to myself for feeling . . .
I surrender to feeling . . .

Take the hand that is over your diaphragm and hold it out about two inches in front of you with an open, relaxed palm. Can you feel the life force flowing through you?

Week 11 affirmation:
Write down your affirmation from the Conscious Creation exercise, say it out loud three times, then write down how it makes you feel . . .

_____
_____

I already get these feelings in these areas of my life (if you can't think of anywhere you get these feelings, guess what your two self-hours are going to be?) . . .

_____
_____

Week 11 (Tuesday)

Time required: the perfect amount for you.

Place a hand over your diaphragm and close your eyes. Take three deep breaths, breathing into the space behind your hand. I feel . . .

_____

_____

_____

_____

Process the uncomfortable emotions:

    I allow myself to feel . . .
    I give myself permission to feel . . .
    I accept that I feel . . .
    The gifts and wisdom of feeling this way are . . .
    I make peace with feeling . . .
    I forgive/apologize to myself for feeling . . .
    I surrender to feeling . . .

Find and hold the connection to your energetic body with your hand about two inches in front of the diaphragm. Observe any uncomfortable emotions that are still present while maintaining your connection to your energetic body.

Week 11 affirmation (taken from Conscious Creation weekend exercise):

_____

_____

_____

_____

I already get these feelings in these areas of my life . . . _____

_____

_____

_____

_____

Week 11 (Wednesday)

Time required: the perfect amount for you.

Place a hand over your diaphragm and close your eyes. Take three deep breaths, breathing into the space behind your hand. I feel . . .

_____

_____

_____

_____

I allow myself to feel . . .

I give myself permission to feel . . .

I accept that I feel . . .

The gifts and wisdom of feeling this way are . . .

I make peace with feeling . . .

I forgive/apologize to myself for feeling . . .

I surrender to feeling . . .

Bring your hand out in front of you and spend a few moments basking in your energetic body. Observe any residual feelings that are not in alignment with who you authentically are and in your mind's eye, release them to recycle back to life force energy.

Week 11 affirmation (taken from Conscious Creation weekend exercise):

_____

_____

_____

_____

I already get these feelings in these areas of my life . . . _____

_____

_____

_____

_____

Week 11 (Thursday)

Time required: the perfect amount for you.

Place a hand over your diaphragm and close your eyes. Take three deep breaths, breathing into the space behind your hand. I feel . . .

_____

_____

_____

_____

Process the uncomfortable emotions:

> I allow myself to feel . . .
> I give myself permission to feel . . .
> I accept that I feel . . .
> The gifts and wisdom of feeling this way are . . .
> I make peace with feeling . . .
> I forgive/apologize to myself for feeling . . .
> I surrender to feeling . . .

Spend a few moments enjoying the vibey bliss of your energetic body with your hand out in front of you. Observe and release with gratitude anything not in alignment with your brilliant, luminous self.

Week 11 affirmation (taken from Conscious Creation weekend exercise):

_____

_____

_____

_____

I already get these feelings in these areas of my life . . . _____

_____

_____

_____

Week 11 (Friday)

Time required: the perfect amount for you.

Place a hand over your diaphragm and close your eyes. Take three deep breaths, breathing into the space behind your hand. I feel . . .

_____

_____

_____

_____

Process the uncomfortable emotions:

> I allow myself to feel . . .
> I give myself permission to feel . . .
> I accept that I feel . . .
> The gifts and wisdom of feeling this way are . . .
> I make peace with feeling . . .
> I forgive/apologize to myself for feeling . . .
> I surrender to feeling . . .

Bliss out in your energetic body with your hand held a few inches in front of the diaphragm. Observe and with loving gratitude, release anything else.

Week 11 affirmation (taken from Conscious Creation weekend exercise):

_____

_____

_____

I already get these feelings in these areas of my life . . . _____

_____

_____

_____

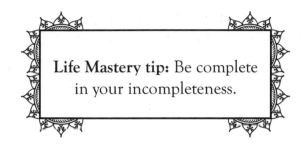

Life Mastery tip: Be complete
in your incompleteness.

Notes & Ideas:

_____
_____
_____
_____
_____
_____
_____
_____
_____
_____
_____
_____
_____
_____
_____
_____
_____
_____
_____
_____
_____
_____
_____

YOUR JOURNEY IS ETERNAL
AND YOUR DESTINATION IS LOVE

Is your mind still messing with you, saying once you arrive at some destination (money, promotion, marriage, kids), then you will be complete? We are meant to feel incomplete. It's this very feeling that pushes us to explore and grow. Feeling incomplete and always reaching for more is the natural state of our eternally expanding energetic being. Recognizing that no external will ever, and is never meant to, complete us internally, is how we surrender into who we authentically are.

Imagine you set out with a friend to drive from Los Angeles to New York, but just out of Las Vegas you decided you would drive forever. Not just to NYC, but to keep on going *always*. How would this change your journey? Would you still be in a rush, or pull over to take a look about? If you ended up on a small side road or took an unexpected detour, would you bitch and moan, or sit back and enjoy the ride? Now imagine the only goal you set on this eternal road trip was to increase your capacity to love. Who would you visit? What sites would you see? What sort of experiences are now on the itinerary? Let's also say the vehicle you get to travel in is a wonder of engineering. The most complex and amazing machine ever built. How would you treat your vehicle? What sort of fuel would you give it? Would you always drive it hard, demanding more and more, or would you really look after it?

YOUR MOST IMPORTANT RELATIONSHIP

Early on in this transformation process, I said we only ever process our perception of reality, through "I feel," never a statement of fact, "I am." When Intuitive Healing students come to the end of their time with me (teaching self-empowerment means pushing you out of the nest when you're ready to fly), this is the last meditation we do. And yes, it is a statement of fact.

Sit comfortably where you will not be interrupted and say the following:

"I am no body."
(repeat three times)

"I am no one."
(repeat three times)

"I am no thing."
(repeat three times)

We are life force energy temporarily inhabiting a physical form. It is only when we fully surrender, that we realize we are every body, every one, and every thing. All forms of life are Source experiencing itself, and through this connection we are all one. Do you follow? We're all in this together! Our tribe is humanity and our home is planet earth. Most of us only come to this realization in the death experience—to have it while living is enlovenment.

WE ARE ALL ONE

Your feelings towards all forms of life speak volumes for how far you've come in connecting with all of who you are. Whether it's snakes, spiders, or sharks, your level of respect for all types of life force energy is a mirror to your own self-respect. If you don't like being out in nature or if there is one particular part of the natural world you reject, be it an animal or a place, it is your mind finding an excuse to hold a part of you separate from experiencing all of who you are. You chose to be human, while the snakes, sharks, and spiders all chose what they were going to be. They knew full well they would be reviled or hunted, but they chose to experience this aspect of life force energy anyway. Who's the more enlightened one now?

You know what your homework is, don't you? Take that part of the natural world you're rejecting or afraid of, and go embrace it. I'm not suggesting picking up deadly snakes or giving a great white a hug. I'm talking about safely putting yourself in a situation where you can reach out and feel the energetic body of whatever it is you've been rejecting. Then, sit in that connection until you move past the initial repulsion or fear to feel the pure positive life force of another being.

Heads up: It's not just animals that are life force energy in physical form. You can reach out and connect with a tree (I recommend it!), a mountain, or a lake. Every physical form is just vibrating energy, and opening up the communication lines not only expands your connection to all life forces you'll also be honoring all life. Remember, the feeling with which you create something exists in your creations. The angry environmentalist, as I once was, is doing more harm than good.

CONSCIOUS RELATIONSHIPS

If there is someone in your life who still seems to push your buttons or someone in your past who was abusive who you don't wish to have any contact with, but speaking your truth would help you to heal and move on, then speaking directly to their energetic self is the way to go. When you speak directly with someone's energetic body, any mental blocks or emotional resistance they have to your message get bypassed.

This ritual is best done at night. Take a bath or shower, letting any energy accumulated during the day wash off. Light a white candle, quiet your mind, and tune into your energetic body. Say out loud, "I wish to speak to the energetic self of . . . (say their full name). (Name), come in peace, come with love, come for healing." You might have to repeat the "invitation" a few times. You should feel a slight shift in the energy. It'll be very subtle, and that daily exercise of tuning into your energetic body will come in handy. When you feel this shift, the other person's energetic self is present. Speak your truth. Whatever it is you want to get off your chest, go for it. Don't worry if you mangle your words or struggle to express yourself, how you feel and the intention behind your words is what will be communicated. It may come to them in a dream or an unconscious inner-knowing depending on how connected they are, but they will eventually get your message. When you've said everything you need to say, thank their energetic self for coming and genuinely offer gratitude that they took the time to help you heal. Then ask them to "go in peace and go with love." You should feel their energetic being leave. As with inviting them in, sometimes you have to (politely) ask them to leave a few times.

A word of warning: If you abuse this ritual, say, by calling in your ex to bitch them out repeatedly, the universe will slap you back BIG TIME.

Ready for me to really bake your noodle? You can also do this with people who have passed away. You don't need a priest or John Edward—we can all speak to the dead. Just don't expect it to be all sunshine and roses. If someone was a miserable git when they were alive, they'll be a miserable git in the afterlife. At least for the first 1–2 years. After enough time in Afterlife School, or whatever it is when we first transition back to nonphysical, they do eventually come around to seeing the brighter side of things.

Story Time: A question I often get asked about "dead people" is, do we go to hell if we suicide? Nope! We go wherever our beliefs think we should go. I lived in a beautiful old apartment in Berlin for many years. Even though I was the only one paying rent I wasn't the only occupant. Some dude had suicided in the bathroom in the 1950s and because of his religious beliefs didn't think he deserved to fully re-emerge with life force energy. Apparently purgatory was my bathroom in Prenzlauer Berg, who knew? I spent many a late night on the loo telling Dude he could move on whenever the fuck he felt like it (and stop creeping me out) but he was so convinced his suicide put him there, when actually *he* was putting himself there, he wouldn't budge. Eventually I stopped trying to move him on out, and would tell him about my day and all the goings on in Germany since 1950. Having a bath the last week I was in that apartment I realized the space was light and clear. For the next few nights I tried to reach out and speak with Dude, but he had finally moved on and fully rejoined life force energy.

CONSCIOUS CREATION

If you work in a profession that seems completely out of alignment with your authentic self, part of your calling might be to raise the vibration in that environment. If you've done your inner work but still feel stuck in an unaligned job, or get offered a promotion you're not sure you want, don't fall into frustration, simply allow your workplace to enjoy some much-needed consciousness (you!) before taking some Inspired Action to move on.

You should now know that what you choose to put your focus and attention on, will create more of it. Do you follow then, that if you continue to only focus on "what is" you'll just continue to create more of what already is? What sometimes confuses students is that at the very beginning of this work, I say to look at exactly where you are and accept it, and now I'm about to tell you to look at where you are . . . and ignore it. The difference between then and now is that you've done your inner work, so there's no subconscious vibrational attraction going on. You are now a Conscious Creator. Yippee!

Just before you fall asleep or when you first wake up, whichever time works best for you, tune into your energetic self. Find that warm fuzzy feeling and say your career or finance goal (the internal one) out loud. Still holding the connection with your energetic body, in your mind's eye imagine how this intention could possibly come to you, how it might realistically show up. Fully feel the excitement of that moment, letting the emotions wash through your entire being. Then say out loud, "this or something better, thank you!" This fun, powerful meditation can be done for any area of your life.

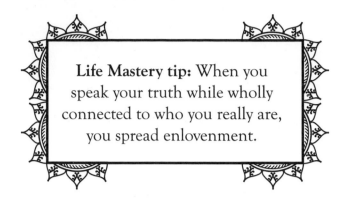

Life Mastery tip: When you speak your truth while wholly connected to who you really are, you spread enlovenment.

Notes & Ideas:

As a problem solver, the mind will always find something to worry about, ad infinitum. Who you really are is much bigger than your mind.

Week 12 (Monday)

Time required: not important.

On a scale of 1–10, how do you feel about where your life is at right now?

_____

Go back to the beginning of the journal. How do the numbers compare?

_____

If where you are today is exactly where you'll be in five years, how does that feel?

_____
_____
_____
_____

Process any uncomfortable emotions, then bask in the vibey goodness that is your energetic body.

Week 12 affirmation: "I am no body. I am no one. I am nothing." When I say this out loud three times, I feel . . .

_____
_____
_____
_____

It's my hunch you'll be on your second go through of this journal before you fully embrace the beauty and grace of this affirmation.

Notes & Ideas:

_____
_____
_____
_____
_____
_____

Week 12 (Tuesday)

Time required: so not important.

I feel . . . _____

_____

_____

_____

_____

Process any uncomfortable emotions that are triggered.

Soak in the bliss that is your energetic body.

Imagine achieving your health and fitness goals. How does it feel?

_____

_____

_____

_____

Week 12 affirmation: "I am no body. I am no one. I am nothing." When I say this out loud three times, I feel . . .

_____

_____

_____

_____

You know any resistance to this universal truth, is ego.

Notes & Ideas:

_____

_____

_____

_____

_____

_____

Week 12 (Wednesday)

Time required: so not important.

I feel . . . _____

_____

_____

_____

_____

Process any uncomfortable emotions that are triggered.

Reach into the aliveness of your energetic body and hold that space for as long as you can.

Imagine your most challenging relationship is now "perfect for you." How does it feel?

_____

_____

_____

_____

Week 12 affirmation: "I am no body. I am no one. I am nothing." When I say this out loud three times, I feel . . .

_____

_____

_____

_____

Only when you fully surrender to this truth, you realize you are every body, every one, and every thing.

Notes & Ideas:

_____

_____

_____

_____

_____

Week 12 (Thursday)

Time required: so not important.

I feel . . . _____

_____

_____

_____

_____

Process any uncomfortable emotions that are triggered.

Bliss out in the warm fuzzies of pure positive life force energy.

Imagine achieving one of your career or financial goals. How does it feel?

_____

_____

_____

_____

Week 12 affirmation: "I am no body. I am no one. I am nothing." Yes, you are. When I say this out loud three times, I feel . . .

_____

_____

_____

_____

Notes & Ideas:

_____

_____

_____

_____

_____

_____

Week 12 (Friday)

Time required: so not important.

I feel . . . _____

_____

_____

_____

_____

Process any uncomfortable emotional triggers.

Chillax in the deliciousness that is your energetic self.

Imagine achieving one of your Lifelong Wishes. How does that feel? What are you wearing? Seeing? Hearing? Who is with you?

_____

_____

_____

_____

_____

_____

Now that you've done your inner work, basking in the feelings of your accomplishment as if it already exists, means you will powerfully align with manifesting it. Congratulations!

Life Mastery affirmation: "I am no body. I am no one. I am nothing." When I say this out loud three times, I feel . . .

_____

_____

_____

_____

CHOOSE YOUR OWN ADVENTURE

This process isn't about handing your power over to something higher. It's about taking it back and being fully responsible for who you are. You chose to come and play physically at this particular moment in earth's history, excited for all the opportunities this time-space reality would offer. You vibrationally matched some of the biggest, shittiest things that have happened in your life for the wisdom and expansion they would present. But, and this is a big *but*, everything is not preordained. There's no old guy in the sky who knows best, granting favors to some while denying others, and deciding how everything will turn out. You get to choose!

When you reconnect to who you really are, you tap in to a wisdom far beyond the mind. You can think of this limitless knowing as a "wise counsel." And as your wise counsel, it's the part that is meant to be running the show. Did you hear that? The intellectual body and emotional body each have their own important function but they should not be your guiding light. Think of the mind like an inner-businessman, all reason and rationalization. While the heart is like a child, full of trust, only ever looking for the best in others. The masculine has a natural affinity with the mind, the feminine with the heart, while self-actualizing enlovenment comes when we honor the masculine and feminine while leading from the energetic body, a.k.a. our intuition and gut feel.

Power was meant to be abused. Ohh yes, it was. The gift of this (there's always a gift!) is that we are meant to be fully responsibility for our own lives. Whether cultural, political, or religious, nothing external should be your final commanding authority. Before anyone clutches their pearls and screams anarchy, when you are fully connected to, and operating from your authentic self, you honor the highest good of everyone and everything . . . because you are every one and every thing.

As you're reading these words, how do you feel? It doesn't actually matter if you're happier or not (now she tells me this?!); the real growth you're looking for is a better connection to who you authentically are:

_____

_____

_____

_____

LET'S TALK ABOUT SEX, BABY . . .

A big part of enjoying the physical expression of your divine self is to enjoy sex. Self sex, partner sex, same sex, group sex, whatever feels honoring and respectful to you. If you have any issues around the wonders of a good shag, your homework this week is to get your sex on and then process any uncomfortable feelings it brings up. Remember I said, doing what makes your heart sing is the easiest way to align with who you really are? Well a mind-blowing orgasm is a close second.

On that note, get your naked bod' in front of a mirror. Light a candle and take a moment to really look at that gorgeous being in front of you. Then say this blessing: "I am so glad I chose you. I love this journey we are on. I am so proud of myself for these steps I've taken to honor my divine being . . ." (Name everything, internal and external, big and small, that you have transformed in the past twelve weeks):

_____

_____

_____

_____

_____

_____

_____

_____

_____

_____

_____

_____

_____

Still looking at yourself in the mirror, "I love all the incredible people with whom I chose to share my journey . . ." Name these people and the gifts they have brought. (You can even name the assholes who were in your life, because we're oh-so-enlightened now.)

_____

_____

_____

Then do something that makes your heart sing. Have a bath, watch the night sky, enjoy some sex (do all three?). Whatever you choose to do, honor your connection to this wondrous planet and celebrate the unique and *amaaazing* being that is *you.*

PUT YOUR OWN OXYGEN MASK ON FIRST

"What about the starving children in Africa?" is a question I sometimes get asked in workshops. You now know that every action you take contains the energy with which you take the action. If you haven't taken the time to clear up your own internal vibration, then everything you touch, including those starving kids in Africa, will be contaminated with your unconsciousness. This isn't selfish or uncaring. You actually care *so* much about others and this incredible planet, that you take care of your *merde* first, because the last thing you want to do is spread it.

Tough Love Time: If you are harder on the women in your life (including daughters), expect more of them, or hold them to a higher standard than you do men, then you are being sexist. Women healing their relationship with themselves is how we transcend misogyny from the inside out. The Sacred Feminine, that aspect of feminine energy in its most exalted form, is fierce, elegant, wild, creative, nurturing, and sensual. Naturally aligned with the emotional body, feminine energy changes constantly, something that can really confuse the masculine. If you chose to inhabit the female form in this lifetime, then your power base lies in embracing the sacred feminine. How you chose to embrace this however, is entirely up to you. Let go of any traditional roles or values you may think of as feminine as they are usually outdated and sexist.

In its healthy form, masculine energy is protective, not possessive. The Sacred Masculine provides because it feels good to provide, not because of any controlling expectation in return. Empowered masculine energy also enjoys competition, not to beat others down but to push themselves to be better. Masculine energy is the more risk-taking, active energy. Being a man of your word, persistence and groundedness are further aspects of the divine masculine. If you are one of those guys who can't sit still, instead of trying to repress your energy with inaction, allow it to flow through you with meditative exercise like martial arts or surfing.

When women embrace the Sacred Feminine in all her beauty and power, the energetic law of balance means this will help men align with the Sacred Masculine in all its grounded action. We are, after all, all in this together!

Sacred Masculine and Feminine Homework: Leaning in to your sacred power base, take your time to consider what healthy, empowered, masculine or feminine feels like to you. Process any uncomfortable triggers this internal aspect of identity brings up. Where in your life do you already have a strong, aligned connection with your sacred masculine/feminine? In what ways, both internal and external, can you continue to support and connect with this empowering energetic aspect of your being?

_____

_____

_____

_____

_____

_____

_____

YOUR DIVINE PHYSICAL SELF

Part of being your own authority means understanding what your unique body needs to stay healthy. What's right for one body may not be right for another. And what's right today may not be what your body needs tomorrow. When we have a loving, respectful connection to our physical selves, it will tell us what it needs and when. I've tried going vegetarian but end up anemic, and even with an iron supplement I run out of energy. My particular physical body needs meat (and wine!). As a conscious creator, my job is to support ethical grazing practices and a way of killing that honors and respects the life I'm responsible for taking.

The fuel you put into the wonder of engineering you inhabit, and how you feel as you prepare it, says a lot about how far you've come on this transformational journey. How we feed ourselves and what we feed ourselves, are aspects of self-love. Your homework this weekend is to go to a farmers' market or organic (a.k.a. high vibration) health food store and buy whatever your body feels like. Have a light meal before you go, so you're not hungry, but not totally full either. If you're wondering about certain foods, hold it or put your hands over it. If the energetic body feels light and open, the food is good for you. If the energetic body feels heavy or closed off, your body doesn't vibe that particular fuel.

NO SUN, NO LIFE

Ancient tribes that worshipped the sun were closer to the truth than many popular religions. The sun is responsible for life on planet earth, so a bit of gratitude is probably due. On the winter and summer solstice (or as close as you can get), get outside in nature and look at everything around you. Marvel at the trees, the flowers, the rivers, and the lakes. Bask in the incredible creative expression you see in front of you. If it's winter, honor the endings you've had in the past year. Winter is the perfect time for putting old things to rest and making room for new growth in the spring. If it's summer, look at all the different forms and all the different colors. All that abundance consciousness right before your eyes. Bow down and revere mother nature as you celebrate the past year.

Here's a bit of trivia you can dazzle your friends with: the expression "many happy returns" comes from the sun, which has returned to the same place in the sky it was in when you were born. One of the most life affirming things you can do is to celebrate your birthday every year. Do not resist your age. Celebrating, big or small, is way of honoring one more year in this physical form, and showing respect and gratitude for this journey you are on.

If there is anything about owning your full power that scares you, do a moon ritual. By honoring the night, you are blessing the shadow aspect that brings balance to all of us. There's nothing to fear in the darker aspects of the human condition. The gold threads interwoven into the unique tapestry that is you couldn't shine bright without the dark lending contrast. When we reject these parts of ourselves (fear is a form of rejection) we reject them in others. Making peace with the parts of yourself that scare you, also means they can't fester and emerge in distorted ways. One of my favorite ways to honor this balancing aspect of who we authentically are is to go on a full moon hike.

Your Bonus Homework is to enjoy as many sunrises, sunsets, and full moons as you can . . . for the rest of your life.

When I tune into pure positive life force energy and ask it to speak to me, this is what it says: love, love.

WHAT IS LOVE?

Generosity, warmth, VULNERABILITY, openness, connection, wonder, courage, kindness, inclusiveness, **freedom,** flexibility, **honesty,** compassion, **fulfillment,** forgiveness, UNDERSTANDING, **patience.** excited, joyous, **GRACIOUS,** optimistic, passionate, playful, ABUNDANT, whole, warmth, gentle, inspired, **braveness.** appreciation, support, empathy, acceptance, quietness, laughter, sharing, creating, LETTING GO, **speaking up,** doing the right thing, being genuine, looking for the best, **WARM FUZZIES** . . . like a multifaceted gem stone, these are only a few of the sides to authentic love. Can you name some more?

_____

_____

_____

_____

_____

_____

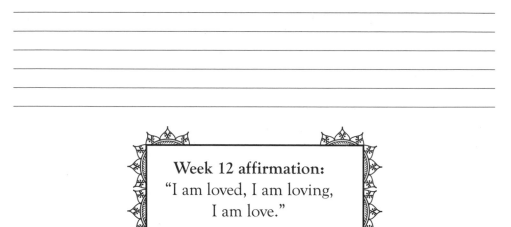

Week 12 affirmation:
"I am loved, I am loving,
I am love."

Set this as true north on your compass as you travel this adventure called life and you will never go wrong.

With authentic love,

Elke Elouise Taylor

Avalon Beach, Australia

Gifts of Some Common Challenging Emotions

Failure: Both success and failure are illusions. You are perfectly where you are meant to be.

Rejection: There isn't anyone who hasn't been rejected by someone, sometime. When you need another person to validate you, you hand your power over to them.

Anger: The great messenger. Your boundaries are being crossed, you're being treated with disrespect OR old emotional wounds are being triggered. Losing your temper (i.e., "road rage") happens when you ignore your anger so it builds up and combines with feeling powerless. Resentment is suppressed anger.

Jealousy: Points out things we want in life, sometimes things that were completely subconscious. Envy is repressed jealousy.

Doubt: Healthy doubt allows us to "think before we jump." Unhealthy doubt is a form of fear.

Fear: Our internal warning system that we are in danger. Healthy fear can save your life. Unhealthy fear (stress) can kill you.

Anxiety: A form of low-level fear. Your internal warning system telling you something is not right.

Guilt: This is the one emotion you don't process! Go below the guilt and identify what you feel, usually manipulated.

List of emotions:

Bliss, freedom, giddy, excited, love, joy, flow, ease, grace, open, wonder, anticipation, smiley, energized, alive, optimistic, enthusiastic, passionate, playful, fulfilled, abundant, vibrant, whole, warm, eager, elegant, spontaneous, quirky, quiet, still, present, reflective, gentle, kind, comfortable, clear, appreciated, accepted, balanced, blessed, calm, secure, accomplished, supported, powerful, creative, feminine, masculine, flexible, inspired, graceful, strong, liberated, light, open-hearted, relaxed, fit, connected, focused, generous, grounded, guided, harmonious, natural, aligned, receptive, sensitive, buoyant, brave, capable, decisive, ready, tolerant, patient, challenged, judgmental, vulnerable, proud, unsettled, disruptive, mind-chatter, frustrated, annoyed, restless, alone, forgotten, distracted, unsupported, nauseous, upset, broken-hearted, worried, doubtful, uncomfortable, uneasy, bruised, cranky, hurt, disrespected, unheard, invisible, unimportant, ignored, judged, worthless, stuck, held-back, tired, powerless, misunderstood, foggy, egotistical, defeated, fear, pain, isolated, failure, disappointed, exhausted, overwhelmed, dumped-on, drained, frightened, stressed, anxiety, not coping, anger, hate, jealousy, desperate, out of control, disturbed, horrified, outraged, terror, abused, violated, envious, unhinged, hysterical.

ACKNOWLEDGMENTS

I usually skip over the author's thank-yous in books. It's only in writing my own I understand the importance of this small piece of gratitude (one of the highest vibrations we can hold, which you've read about by now). I owe a debt of gratitude to all the Intuitive Healing students over the past fifteen years. You know who you are, you brave, beautiful people! I'm especially grateful to those who come for tarot readings in Los Angeles, which is how I began to honor this unique expression of myself and walk my soul's true path. I have been well supported physically, emotionally, and spiritually on this incredible journey called life; a big, big thank you to: Ada, Beau, Georgia, Malinda, Nicole, Heidi, Jessica, Karina, Gillian, Skye, Emma, Tal, Michael, Deanna, Halla, Kartika, Flora, Midge, Tina, Leah, Strachan, Scot, Sasha, mum, dad, and my grandfather Wac from whose side I inherited this gift.